Pioneers of Aerial Combat

> *To Lewis.*
> *I didn't know you could miss someone so much.*

Other books by Michael Foley

Front-Line Essex – Sutton, 2005
Front-Line Kent – Sutton, 2006
Essex, Ready For Anything – Sutton, 2006
Hard As Nails – Spellmount, 2007
Front-Line Suffolk – Sutton, 2007
Front-Line Thames – History Press, 2008
More Front-Line Essex – History Press, 2008
Essex in the First World War – History Press, 2009
Prisoners of the British – Bank House Books, 2009
Essex at War Through Time – Amberley, 2009
London Under Attack – History Press, 2010
London Through Time – Amberley, 2010
Havering Through Time – Amberley, 2010
Barking and Dagenham Through Time – Amberley, 2010
London's East End Through Time – Amberley, 2011
Disasters on the Thames – History Press, 2011
Essex Through Time – Amberley, 2012
Essex at War in Old Photographs – Amberley, 2012

Pioneers of Aerial Combat

Air Battles of the First World War

Michael Foley
www.michael-foley-history-writer.co.uk

Pen & Sword
AVIATION

First published in Great Britain in 2013 by
Pen & Sword Military
an imprint of
Pen & Sword Books Ltd
47 Church Street
Barnsley
South Yorkshire
S70 2AS

ISBN 978 1 78159 272 4

A CIP catalogue record for this book is available from the British
Library

Typeset in Ehrhardt by
Mac Style, Bridlington, East Yorkshire
Printed and bound in the UK by CPI Group (UK) Ltd, Croydon,
CRO 4YY

Pen & Sword Books Ltd incorporates the imprints of Pen & Sword
Archaeology, Atlas, Aviation, Battleground, Discovery, Family
History, History, Maritime, Military, Naval, Politics, Railways,
Select, Social History, Transport, True Crime, and Claymore Press,
Frontline Books, Leo Cooper, Praetorian Press, Remember When,
Seaforth Publishing and Wharncliffe.

For a complete list of Pen & Sword titles please contact
PEN & SWORD BOOKS LIMITED
47 Church Street, Barnsley, South Yorkshire, S70 2AS, England
E-mail: enquiries@pen-and-sword.co.uk
Website: www.pen-and-sword.co.uk

Contents

Acknowledgement

Thank you to Linne Matthews for all her hard work in editing this book. And thanks also to James Payne of Through their Eyes (www.throughtheireyes2. co.uk) for the use of his photographs.

Note on illustrations

Introduction

The world of the early aircraft has always been something that has fascinated me, which is one of the reasons I have come to write this book. The courage of those early pioneers of flight was incredible; they risked their lives in what were often machines held together by bits of string and wood. When they took off they didn't know if their aircraft would hold together until they landed or whether the engine would continue to run once they were off the ground.

I find it amazing how flight evolved so quickly from those early flimsy machines into the faster, more reliable aircraft that within little more than a decade of the first flights were performing incredible acts of flying in the conflict of the First World War. It is, of course, an accepted fact that the rapid progression in the art of flying was mainly due to the outbreak of the war. Governments would not have been willing to spend so much money on the development and production of aircraft in peacetime. This was especially true of the British Government, who in the early years of flight lagged behind other powers in the use of flying machines and was totally unprepared for the war when it began. Private producers of aircraft would also not have put as much effort into developing new aircraft if they did not have such a ready market for their wares.

According to an early copy of *The War Illustrated* magazine, the French did more to improve their military aviation in the first two weeks of the war than they had done in the previous two years of peace, and this was despite France being one of the leading countries in the development of early flight.

There has obviously been much written about early flight since the First World War. Much of the research for this book has come from what was written at the time by those involved, including features in newspapers and periodicals. Of course, this has to be taken in the light of how much of what was reported was propaganda. I have, however, tried to present a balanced view of events.

One of the most surprising aspects of the organization of flight during the war was the dispute over who should have been in charge of organizing the supply of aircraft. The early years of the war were marked by fierce competition between the Royal Flying Corps (RFC) and the Royal Naval Air Service (RNAS) as both arms of the flying service tried to outdo each other in obtaining the best aircraft in the greatest numbers.

When the government did try and do something about the situation it seems that the men and groups given the task were unable to force both sides into an agreement – often due to the fact that they had no power to do so. Throughout the war there were a number of committees formed by the government to do just this but none were given sufficient powers to carry out the task. There also seemed to be little government stomach for a fight with the Admiralty, who appeared to be intent on obtaining for themselves the best aviation materials available, even if this was at the expense of the war effort as a whole.

The disputes also carried on in later years between the Air Board and the Ministry of Munitions over who was the most qualified to take control of aircraft production. There are a number of reports available in The National Archives from both of these organizations that seem to show them trying to outdo each other and argue their own case – perhaps often at the expense of what was the best action for the war effort.

An obviously very popular aviation meet, going by the size of the crowd. Unfortunately, there is no location of the picture given on this postcard.

I have concentrated on events that took place in England and on the Western Front in relation to aviation during the war. There were, of course, other theatres of war where flying took place during the conflict and no doubt much of what I have written would also apply to the situation in these places, but perhaps that is something for another time.

Michael Foley
Romford, 2013

Chapter 1

Early Years of Flight

The beginning of the twentieth century was a significant time in the development of manned flight. There had been numerous attempts at flight in the early years of the century, mostly unsuccessful and many fatal for those who attempted it. The greatest level of success seemed to be with gliders. This was no doubt due to the lack of reliable engines.

In the early twentieth century, Gustave Whitehead, a German living in America, claimed that he and a passenger had made a half-mile powered flight. Another German, Karl Jatho, had a motor glider that supposedly hopped for about 60 metres at a height of 3 metres. This was months before the Wright brothers' first flight. However, what is now recognized as the first powered flight took place on 17 December 1903, when the Wright brothers made a number of powered flights, the longest being of fifty-seven seconds.

1 LATHAM en plein vol

Hubert Latham was one of the most successful early aviators and flew at Blackpool.

WRIGHT BIPLANE.

Recognized as the first men to fly, this image shows the Wright brothers' biplane.

Where the Wright brothers succeeded over the other early claimants was that they had recognized proof of their success.

The biggest problem for aviators at the time was in building an aircraft engine that did not fail after a minute or two in flight. It was a problem that the Wright brothers began to solve. By the end of 1905 they had made a flight lasting thirty-nine minutes.

As early as 1904, a member of the British Army, Lieutenant Colonel John Capper, spoke to the Wright brothers about providing aircraft to the British Government. The early interest was not followed up and British interest in aviation began to lag behind from that point.

Even the Wright brothers' own American government were not interested in their machines. It was the French who showed the most awareness of the prospects of flight. There had been a thriving flight industry in France for years, again mainly unsuccessful. The Wright brothers went to France in 1907 and made a number of flights that led to the rapid development of flying in the country. One of their customers was the first Englishman to fly, Griffith Brewer. By this time, the Americans were also showing more interest.

In August 1908 Wilbur Wright flew an aircraft for two minutes and travelled three times round the Hunaudières racecourse at Le Mans in France. In July 1909, Blériot, a Frenchman, became the first man to fly across the English Channel. Attempts at flight were taking place in many parts of the civilized world. Interest had also grown in England by this time, especially in Dagenham.

Despite the formation of the flying ground at Dagenham, the first recognized powered flight in England took place at Farnborough. The pilot was Samuel Franklin Cody, an American who on 16 October 1908 flew almost 1,400 feet at a height of 18 feet.

As with the Wright brothers' claims to have made the first powered flight in the world, there were other claims to have been the first to fly in England. Albert Roe began flying at Brooklands in 1908. He had a shed there where he kept his aircraft. In June 1908 he was taxiing when he realized he was off the ground. He supposedly flew for 150 feet. There were no official observers of the event but two workers at Brooklands had seen him. However, his success was never recognized by the Aeronautical Society.

The *Barking, East Ham & Ilford Advertiser* ran an article in 1909 under the headline 'Monsters of the Air at Dagenham'. The story was related to a site acquired by the Aeronautical Society of Great Britain next to the river Thames in Dagenham. It was described as a lonely, isolated spot on the Dagenham Marshes – the ideal place for those engaged in secret experiments with flying machines.

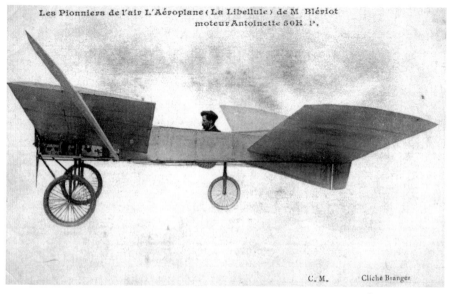

Blériot's Dragonfly, built in 1907. It had a 50hp engine.

Strangely enough, very few of the books on early flying mention the Dagenham site, perhaps because it was so short-lived and not very successful, but it was actually the first organized flying ground in England.

The decision was made to use Dagenham after a meeting by the Aeronautical Society in December 1908. A committee was formed to find an experimental ground. It had to be isolated to keep what was going on there secret, while also being easy to reach. The ground at Dagenham had water on three sides: the Thames, Dagenham Breach and a canal. The rent was £50 a year and donations of £218 18s 6d were raised towards running it. The land was leased from Samuel Williams, who had created an industrial area around Dagenham Dock. There were already some buildings on the site but others were erected to house the aircraft.

The spot was not quite as isolated or as secret as the newspaper story led people to believe. Dagenham Dock Railway Station had already been opened the year before, funded by Samuel Williams.

The machines were not really secret, either, although the supposedly remote area did go some way to deterring large crowds from gathering to watch attempted flight. However, in August 1909, a journalist from the *Essex Weekly News* was invited to inspect the machines during a private show for members of the society.

Some of the pilots at Dagenham were well-known figures. Major Baden Powell, brother of the defender of Mafeking, built a quadraplane there. The major's machine had a petrol tank capable of holding a gallon of petrol – enough for an hour's flight. (Aeroplanes of the time were obviously not the fuel guzzlers of today.) The major had been one of the committee that had decided on the location of the ground.

There was also a monoplane at the airfield, built by a J.E. Neale, an electrical engineer who was lodging at Dagenham Village. It was similar to Blériot's machine and was entered for the London to Manchester Race, which had a first prize of £10,000.

Another inventor at the site was C.A. Moreing, who had made his money from gold mining in Australia. There were also two other Australians at the site, F.J. Healey and A.J. Roberts. Moreing conducted trials of a gyroscope at Dagenham. The three Australians stayed on after the site closed and conducted some remote-control experiments.

The site had hangars and a clubhouse. One of the hangars was built to hold a balloon. It was constructed by West and Co, now well-known undertakers in the area but then also involved in the building trade. According to Jack

One of the early unusual-looking aircraft. This one was at Brooklands, where those on the ground would lay on the floor to see if any light could be seen between the aircraft and the ground.

West, of the second generation of the family business, in his book *Personal Memories of Dagenham Village: 1920 Onwards*, this hangar was built as early as 1903 but other sources state that it was unfinished when the site opened in 1909.

There were soon problems at Dagenham. The ground was quite rough and there were plans to flatten it and lay out firmer sections for wheeled vehicles. It seems, however, that not enough members used the site to make this practical. Some of those who did use it described it as a weed preserve, and local fishermen accused the members of scaring the fish with their machines.

Some of the men involved in flying would not have been out of place in the film about early aviators, *Those Magnificent Men in Their Flying Machines*. Others were serious inventors. Perhaps the most famous name in aviation history connected with the Dagenham site was Frederick Handley Page. He built several aeroplanes at the Dagenham field and at other local sites, including nearby Barking Creek.

Page's real success in aviation came elsewhere. There seems to be some dispute over whether it was Handley Page or the Short brothers who founded the first British public company to build aircraft. In 1911, Handley Page built the 0/100, the largest plane in Britain at the time. In 1912, Page moved to Cricklewood, where he built planes for use in the First World War.

The Dagenham airfield was, it seems, empty by the end of 1909. The Aeronautical Club of Great Britain had already opened its own airfield near Leysdown, on the Isle of Sheppey in Kent. Short Brothers had opened their aircraft factory close by, while Dagenham's part in early flight was soon forgotten.

The Manchester Guardian reported in March 1909 that the Aeronautical Club of Great Britain was rushing to complete its aerodrome at Shellbeach to have the formal opening in April. An exhibition was planned for the opening and the secretary, Mr Harold Perrin, said that the War Office had approached the Wright brothers to give a demonstration of their flying, which he hoped would take place at the new aerodrome later in the year.

Flying was not confined to the Aeronautical Club sites. After a successful flying week in Rheims, France, there were calls for a similar event to take place in England. In September 1909, *The Penny Illustrated Paper* reported that Blackpool could be the site of the English Flying Week. Its great stretch of sand was the ideal place for flying and more than £6,000 in prize money had already been promised to attract well-known names in aviation.

A postcard showing the aircraft at Blackpool Flying Week, which was held in October 1909.

Alderman John Bickerstaffe and Mr Parkinson, members of the Blackpool Corporation, and Huntley Walker, chairman of the Lancashire Aeronautical Club, met with the committee of the Aeronautical Club of Great Britain on 3 September to agree details of the flying week. It was to take place between 18 and 23 October.

The idea of a flying week was not confined to Blackpool. Doncaster was also chosen as a possible site. It was claimed that the racecourse and the stand there was the best location for a flying week, with an open plain for flying and good railway transport for the spectators. It was argued that it

Louis Paulhan at Blackpool in his new Vulture biplane. He flew 28 kilometres in a strong wind.

would outshine the Blackpool week. Strangely, it was then decided to hold the Doncaster meeting at the same time as the Blackpool one. It is very apparent that competition in regard to flying began at an early stage and carried on for some time.

There were attempts by the Aeronautical Club of Great Britain to get the organizers of the Doncaster meeting to delay until after the Blackpool event but they were unsuccessful. There was then a scramble to get the most famous aviators to attend each meeting. The only concession agreed was that, while Blackpool would include flying competitions with prizes, Doncaster would be an exhibition with aviators paid just for appearing. The result was that both events were well attended, although some days were less successful due to bad weather conditions.

The success of the flying weeks at Blackpool and Doncaster had awakened once again the possibility of the use of aircraft for military purposes. The advances in flying had put an end to the belief that flying was too dependent on good weather. The authorities were now convinced that the military use of flight could go beyond the use of balloons, which had been quite successful for the military.

There had been trials with balloons on Salisbury Plain and the Germans had also been carrying out similar experiments. It was found that small arms fire had little effect on balloons – a lesson that was soon proved when the war began and aircraft attempted to shoot down the German airships that were bombing the country. It was only artillery that managed to destroy large balloons. The problem at the time was that there were no guns that could fire vertically. The artillery weapons available could only fire at a low angle.

Leon Delarange in his monoplane with a Gnome engine, at Doncaster.

Roger Sommer at Doncaster, where he won the award for flying 97 miles.

The Aeronautical Club later moved to a site at Eastchurch in Kent, which went from strength to strength. In *The Times* in March 1910, there were reports on the flying taking place there, when the Honourable C.S. Rolls made a few short flights while a Mr Grace, in his Short Wright biplane, rose to a height of 220 feet. The club became the Royal Aeronautical Club in 1910.

Samuel Cody – known as Colonel Cody – took British citizenship at the Doncaster meeting but, as the image shows, he had little luck flying there.

Not all newspapers saw the craze for flying as a sensible one. In April 1910, *The Penny Illustrated Paper* described the situation as: 'Fools have already begun to step in'. The article went on to say, 'Last autumn there had only been thirty men in the world who could fly. Now, with aircraft costing no more than a few hundred pounds, there are 300.'

The view of the newspapers seemed to be born out when in July 1910 C.S. Rolls was killed at Bournemouth. At the time of his death he was rated as one of the top two or three most capable British aviators. His plane dropped to the ground while he was trying to land on a target; he was thrown out and broke his neck. Rolls had already made a closer landing to the target than Claude Grahame-White, who was also a well-known aviator, but had wanted to improve on his first attempt.

Later that year in October, four pilots were killed within the month. These included Mentes and Blanchard. Blanchard was the twenty-sixth aviator to die in two years.

By this time, the Aeronautical Club had moved to their new premises at Eastchurch. Short Brothers had been building aircraft at their old site and they later also moved to premises near Eastchurch. They were by this time building machines designed by the Wright brothers. In 1911 they built the first twin-engine plane, the S.39.

Flying could be dangerous in its early days but was also very profitable for those skilled at it. It was reported in October 1909 that in the previous ten weeks £100,000 in prize money had been divided between the top nine fliers. Most of the money came from foreign meetings but there had been two in England – at Doncaster and Blackpool. The men were named as Henri Farman, Hubert Latham, Henri Rougier, Roger Sommer, the Wright brothers – Orville and Wilbur, Louis Paulhan, Louis Blériot and Glenn Curtiss.

Eastchurch Aerodrome, where much of the early flying in the country took place, including naval flying.

The Wright brothers with Mr Horace Short, of Short Brothers, following them.

The report went on to explain that not only was prize money available to the men but they often gave flying lessons, which was very lucrative for them. Some of the nine also made and sold their own aircraft. The prices of the machines were: Blériot monoplane, £400; Farman biplane, £1,000; Voisin biplane, £1,050; Antoinette monoplane, £1,000; and a Wright machine, £1,000.

There was a military connection at Eastchurch, which was to see the beginning of the air arm of the forces when, in December 1910, the Aeronautical Club offered the use of two aircraft at the site for the benefit of naval officers from Sheerness and Chatham. Admiral Sir C.C. Drury, Commander-in-Chief, The Nore, stated that the most modern type of biplanes with Gnome

Short Brothers' early factory at Eastchurch.

engines were at the disposal of naval officers without charge, although they had to join the club first and pay for any damages incurred. The Admiralty decided that men selected for flying should be paid for the exceptional nature of their duties. Those from the Navy willing to fly were to be paid an extra allowance of six shillings a day for officers, two shillings and sixpence for petty officers and two shillings for able seamen.

In March 1910, the Aero Show took place at Olympia. There was an interesting claim made by the London Aviation Company regarding their monoplane, the Ornis, which was on display and for sale. It said that flight was guaranteed.

A postcard showing Claude Grahame-White, one of the best-known names in British aviation, inspecting one of his early aircraft.

Flying was also taking place elsewhere and the £10,000 prize that had been offered by the *Daily Mail* in 1907 for a flight from London to Manchester was finally claimed in April 1910 by Louis Paulhan, a Frenchman who had made the two allowed stops on the way. An English attempt was made at the same time by Grahame-White and despite the fact that he lost, the publicity did much to encourage English fliers. Lord Northcliffe, owner of the *Mail*, had been offering flying prizes to encourage flying in this country, which was still at that time lagging behind other powers. Also in the same month, a Mr Rudley made four flights in a monoplane at Huntingdon Aerodrome and twice travelled 1¼ miles.

In February 1911, Mr Grahame-White made several flights with a new biplane at Hendon Aerodrome. It was built to his own design. Grahame-White also owned a 50hp Blériot, which was flown by a Mr Hamel. A number of other flights took place at Hendon over the same weekend.

In April 1911, the Air Battalion of the Royal Engineers was formed. There had been a School of Ballooning for some years and a balloon factory had been established at Farnborough in 1905. This became the headquarters of the Air Battalion 1st Company. No. 1 Company was based at Farnborough and was equipped with airships and commanded by Captain Edward Maitland. No. 2 Company was commanded by Captain John Fulton and was based at Larkhill, on Salisbury Plain, and was equipped with aircraft.

There was a description of Hendon Aerodrome printed in *The Times* in May 1911. It comprised 270 acres, with a row of aeroplane sheds to its southern edge. Based at the site were ten Blériot monoplanes, four Farman

Marcel Desoutter in his Bleriot, being aided by a policeman and others holding down the aircraft while he runs the engine.

biplanes, two of them of the military type, two Grahame-White biplanes, one Howard Wright biplane and several Valkyries, one of which could carry three people.

The *Daily Mail* was obviously still keen on promoting flight and they were holding another air race in July 1911, with a prize of £10,000. The competition also led to an example of the regulation that had begun to appear in relation to flying. Douglas Graham Gilmour was to take part in the race but was called to appear before the Aeronautical Club. They then revoked Mr Gilmour's flying licence for dangerous flying over Henley while on a flight from Brooklands to Henley at the time of the regatta. It seems that the Aeronautical Club rules were that flying over towns or highly populated areas was seen as unnecessary and dangerous. This also added little to the development of flight. Mr Gilmour argued that they could not revoke his licence as it had been issued by the French Aeronautical Club.

The matter was eventually dealt with in the courts but Gilmour's ban was upheld as the court decided that the Aeronautical Club of Great Britain had jurisdiction over flying in Britain no matter who had issued a pilot's licence.

Another aircraft factory began production in January 1912, when the Coventry Ordnance Company decided to establish an aviation department. The managing director, Rear Admiral Bacon, stated that a new type of biplane

Not all early aircraft were successful, as seen on this postcard showing one crash-landed in a lake.

would be built and that the company had engaged Mr Thomas Sopwith, a man whose name was to become well known in flying. The company were not planning to open their own aerodrome as testing would be carried out at Brooklands.

Flying was taking place in numerous locations by this time and often drew large crowds of spectators. Early aviators still had problems with their machines. A Henri Salmet attempted to fly from London to Paris in 1912. Unfortunately, his engine stopped and he was forced to land in a field at Roman Road, East Ham. In the same year, a naval biplane crashed in an onion field in Barking. The pilot, Thomas Waket, was taken to East Ham Hospital.

Fortunately, it was not only crashing planes that the public were to experience. The popularity of flying was evident when thousands of spectators turned up at a garden fete and aeroplane display at Hylands in Essex in aid of Woodford schools. This was followed by a display in Barking Park, when a reported 30,000 to 40,000 spectators turned up to see Mr B.C. Hucks fly his military-type Blériot plane. The display was arranged to raise money for the foundation of a cottage hospital in Barking.

There was an important development in military flying in March 1912. An announcement was made in Parliament by Colonel Seely and Winston

A Henri Farman F20 with a 70hp or 80hp Le Rhone engine. This craft was taken by the Central Flying School in 1914.

The route of an air race in 1913. It started and finished at Hendon, London, and thirteen competitors took part.

Churchill on the subject of flying. It seemed that the government had finally begun to take flying seriously and had decided that the Army and Navy were to be equipped with the human and mechanical equipment of aerial warfare to bring them up to the standard of other great powers.

The Royal Flying Corps, with a naval and a military arm, was formed in April 1912. This would eventually lead to the abolition of the Air Battalion, which was amalgamated into the RFC in May.

There was to be a School of Aviation, where both army and naval officers would be taught to fly. At the time, the French military already had more than 200 aircraft and the Germans were thought to have about the same, but this was a badly kept secret. One of the things that was said to be lacking in Britain was landing places and it was to be hoped that private flying schools would allow their grounds to be used by the military. The plan, according to Colonel Seely, was that the military officers should learn to fly at private schools before going to the new Central Flying School. The Central Flying School would teach those able to fly how to fly as a military pilot, not a civilian one.

The plan was to provide the military with 131 aircraft, but this would not be possible straight away for the simple reason that there were not enough aircraft available. It was hoped that seventy-one would be available in the first year, but even this number seemed optimistic when one considers the actual number of aircraft being made at the time.

Further details began to be released by the government in the following weeks. The plans were based on the recommendations of a committee presided over by Colonel Seely. They had made it clear that by this time flying was beyond the experimental stage. As well as the actual members of the new unit there would also be a large reserve force.

The naval wing of the Flying Corps would remain at Eastchurch for the time being. The existing Army Aircraft Factory at Farnborough would be renamed the Royal Aircraft Factory. As well as making aircraft, the factory would train mechanics and carry out experimental work.

The aircraft used by the Navy at Eastchurch were mainly built by Shorts. Others were added later. One company that built planes at Brooklands was the Universal Aviation Company Ltd. It had the nickname of the Universal Destruction Company Ltd., because the planes they built tended to crash. Part of Eastchurch was rented as a naval flying station and experiments on seaplanes were carried out from there.

The first instance of a flight taking off from a ship took place at Sheerness and wasn't very successful. The plane landed on the sea but then couldn't take off again. Work on airships had been put on hold after the *Mayfly* disaster of September 1911, when the airship broke in half, but was revived when it became clear how well Germany were doing with their airships. (*Mayfly* was the first British rigid airship. It was demolished by strong winds in September 1911, before it even took its first flight.)

A number of other air stations were planned along the East Coast and one opened on Kent's Isle of Grain in December 1912. There was also to be an airship station there as the Navy had bought airships from France. A station at Kingsnorth in Kent opened in April 1914.

Another connection with private enterprise was that a rent should be paid to private aerodromes for landing rights and the use of their sheds. The Central Flying School would be on Salisbury Plain, near Upavon in Wiltshire. Thirty aircraft had been ordered for the Central Flying School and twelve hydroplanes for Eastchurch.

By the end of April 1912, the rates of pay for the new Royal Flying Corps had been established, with a squadron commander on twenty-five shillings a day, a flight commander on seventeen shillings a day, a flying officer on twelve shillings a day and the commandant of the flying school on £12,000 per annum.

In May, the first commander of the Flying School was appointed. It was Captain Godfrey M. Paine RN. Paine was forty years old and had been in the Royal Navy since 1885. He was the captain of HMS *Actaeon*, based at Sheerness. The first naval fliers at Eastchurch had been listed on the books of the *Actaeon* so he had nominally already been commander of Eastchurch. Under Paine were Lieutenant (Acting Commander) C.R. Salmon RN, in charge of the Naval Wing, and Captain F.H. Sykes, in charge of the Military Wing.

By June, the construction of the Central Flying School was well underway. The sheds had been erected and the lecture rooms and barracks were having electricity fitted. The school was expected to be complete by August and the commanding officers had already moved in.

A competition to decide which aircraft would be used at the school was held at Larkhill, near Bristol Flying School. A squadron of the RFC was being formed there under Captain H.R.M. Brooke-Popham of the Oxford and Bucks Light Infantry. A number of Royal Engineers were included and two of them had already qualified as pilots.

Despite the advances in the design of aircraft they were still dangerous and there were fatalities. One of these was Edward Petre, a member of a well-known Essex family. Petre was attempting to fly from Brooklands to Edinburgh in December 1912. He had already flown more than 250 miles but ran into a strong wind over the Yorkshire coast, which caused his aircraft to crash, killing him instantly.

The aircraft was a Martin Handasyde monoplane. Petre was attempting to make the flight non-stop. He was seen over Whitby, where the strong wind was understood as being dangerous to the flight. The aircraft then

The Royal Engineers played an important part in early military flight. The member marked on the right of the group of engineers shown on this postcard was killed in a flying accident.

came down near Redcar Road at Marske. A policeman was the first on the scene and the body was removed to the Miners' Hospital at Marske.

Further air stations were opened in early 1913 by the Navy, and one was at Great Yarmouth. One of the reasons the site was chosen was the availability of coastguard cottages for the men stationed there, as there was not enough money to build accommodation. Other men based at the site lived in the town.

The airfield quickly became a tourist attraction and was promoted by the local press. Locals were given flights as passengers. There was some security at the site at night; a naval pensioner and his dog. The first aircraft there was a Maurice Farman biplane built by the Aircraft Manufacturing Company

The first recruit of the Royal Flying Corps!

A humorous postcard of the first recruit to the Royal Flying Corps. He had no need of an aircraft, having his own wings.

at Hendon. Another station was opened at Felixstowe in Suffolk, but was sometimes known as Harwich.

There were attempts to form independent flying corps alongside the government forces. One of these was suggested at a meeting at Liverpool Town Hall in May 1913. Local businessmen and ship owners had offered to finance the setting up of a Liverpool flying corps. It seems that this was common practice in other European countries at the time. It was also to become quite common in the war in relation to infantry battalions. The offer was to provide two aircraft, and the agreement of the War Office had been sought.

Another meeting was held in Liverpool the following week and was attended by the now Major Sykes, commanding the Military Wing of the RFC. He brought with him a letter from Colonel Seely stating that it would be a mistake to establish local corps apart from the central organization.

The letter went on to explain that membership of the RFC was open to all, including civilians, and that anyone could apply to join. The government could not accept gifts of aircraft if there were restricted conditions attached to their use. They would, however, accept a contribution towards aerial defence. The cost of setting up a squadron of the RFC was £40,000, which would provide eighteen aircraft, transport and other accessories.

There was another death from flying in June 1913. This time it was at Brooklands. A plane was circling the airfield at about 80 miles per hour at a height of about 30 feet when it banked too steeply and hit the ground. The pilot, Gordon Bell, was seriously injured, but his passenger, Lieutenant James Robert Branch Kennedy of the naval section of the RFC, was killed. The plane was a Martin Handasyde monoplane of 120hp. It was the same make of plane in which Edward Petre had been killed a few months earlier.

By July 1913, there had been some changes. What had been known as Hydro aeroplanes became known as seaplanes. It was obvious that more work was needed on these as up to this point they were just aircraft with floats. There were also large naval manoeuvres taking place in July and it was the first time that aircraft had been in use with the fleet. They were to prove how useful they could be for reconnaissance but this was mainly possible only for aircraft fitted with wireless telegraph.

It was also becoming clear that the Navy needed different types of aircraft to the Army: fighting seaplanes to work from ships; scouting seaplanes to work with the fleet; and home service fighting planes to protect Britain and

Postcard showing Samuel Cody's aircraft. Cody was one of the early pioneers of flight in Britain, despite being an American.

patrol the coast. It was to be the different objectives of the naval aircraft that were to lead to many of the problems that occurred when the war began.

Developments in aviation were coming thick and fast in the last few years before the First World War. One of these was an air ambulance, which was built by S.F. Cody at Farnborough. It was a large biplane, which Cody was planning to use in the Waterplane Race round the coast, which had a £5,000 prize offered by the *Daily Mail*. The aircraft had a 60-foot wingspan, was to have seating accommodation for two surgeons and carry apparatus for use in a field hospital. A portable operating table had been invented for the plane by Lieutenant Colonel J.F. Donegan RAMC.

There were also several other flying competitions before the First World War. An air derby was held in September 1913. Fourteen competitors took off from Hendon to fly around London. The turning points were at West Thurrock and Epping. Each competitor had to land three times for their number to be recorded as proof of completing the course.

Experimentation in flying was not only restricted to building aeroplanes. One of the first parachute jumps was made from an aeroplane at Farnborough on 18 October 1913. The parachutist was Major E.M. Maitland, who was a member of the Essex Regiment. Despite the success of the jump, parachutes

Colonel Cody, credited as the first man to fly in England.

were not to become part of an airman's kit for many years. They were hardly used at all during the war.

Flying may have progressed in the period just before the war began but it was still very dangerous. In May 1914, two RFC airmen were killed in an accident. Lieutenant John Empson, the pilot, and his mechanic, George Cudmore, were killed when their BE (Blériot Experimental) biplane crashed into a hedge. BE biplanes were built by the Royal Aircraft Factory, and a number of types were used during the war.

They were part of a flight of ten aircraft of No. 2 Squadron being taken from Montrose to Salisbury Plain. They hit a patch of fog near Northallerton. The journey was being carried out in stages and they had been on the Seaton Carew to York stage. Two other aircraft in the flight were damaged when landing but there were no other fatalities. The two deaths brought the number of deaths of army airmen to nine so far in 1914.

The extension of RFC flying bases took place before the war began. One of these was to be at Orford Ness in Suffolk. Orford Ness is an island just off the coast in the North Sea and had to be purchased from its owner. The price for the island was decided by arbitration as the owner, Lord Rendlesham, and the government could not agree on the cost. The airfield was to be used for secret experiments. It was an ideal spot for this as, being an island it was remote from the public. Orford Ness continued to be a secret military site up until the nuclear age.

By this time, there were also eight naval air stations. These were at Calshot, Dundee, Eastchurch, Felixstowe, Fort Grange, Killingholme, Great Yarmouth and the Isle of Grain. There were two advance stations, at Clacton and Westgate, and two airship stations, at Kingsnorth and Farnborough. The Navy now had forty aircraft, thirty-one seaplanes and seven airships.

Chapter 2

Early Aircraft Producers

This chapter covers some of the early aircraft makers, listed in order of when each company began production. It is not an exhaustive list as that would make for a much longer book.

It was estimated that during the First World War more than a 1,000 companies played some part in the production of aircraft. Appendix 2 has a more detailed list of wartime aircraft producers, although again not a complete list.

In its attempt to supply the Air Battalion with aircraft, the British Government was criticized as early as the end of 1910 for ignoring British aircraft makers. They had mainly been buying French aircraft, especially the Paulhan. Although there was criticism of the government it is probably true that at this time the French were producing better aircraft than the few British manufacturers that existed. The reasons for this were not just due to their lead in design and manufacturing. French aircraft makers were promised that suitable machines would be purchased by their government in high enough numbers to make their development worthwhile. British producers did not have this incentive. In fact, if anything, the British Government was also promoting French makers by buying large numbers of aircraft from them.

There was a report in *The Observer* in October 1911 that an offer was to be made to the British aircraft industry by the government. This was not, however, an offer to buy the aircraft they were making; it was to produce an aircraft that was of a certain degree of efficiency, which would point to the government belief that what they were already producing did not match up to this standard.

The situation did not improve and although in March 1912 Winston Churchill stated that the planes for the Navy had been made principally in England, the quality was still not good. This was shown when Colonel Seeley said that the War Office could not purchase British machines at the price of human lives.

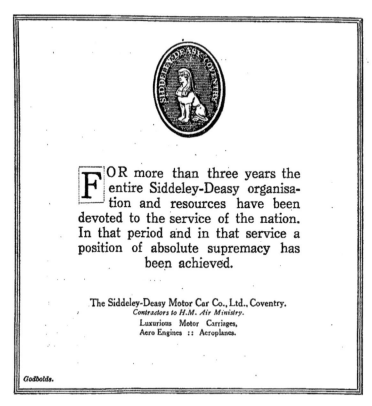

FOR more than three years the entire Siddeley-Deasy organisation and resources have been devoted to the service of the nation. In that period and in that service a position of absolute supremacy has been achieved.

The Siddeley-Deasy Motor Car Co., Ltd., Coventry.
Contractors to H.M. Air Ministry.
Luxurious Motor Carriages,
Aero Engines :: Aeroplanes.

Godbolds.

A number of companies produced parts for aircraft and complete aircraft, as this Siddeley-Deasy advert shows.

According to *The Observer* in March 1912, any British aircraft manufacturer offering an aircraft to the government was ignored if the aircraft did not have a French Gnome or Renault engine. This was despite there being a reliable British engine, the Green, which had won awards in the Alexander Aero Motor Competition the month before.

Just as flying was much more popular in other countries than in Britain in the early days, aircraft production followed similar lines. Most early aircraft were foreign, and even when made in Britain they were often produced in foreign-owned factories. This was evident at the Olympia Air show in February 1913, where there were twenty-six full-size aircraft on show. Of these, nineteen were British-made, but five of them were of foreign design and made in the British factories of French aircraft makers. Of the nineteen British-made aircraft, only one had a British engine, a Wolseley in a Vickers biplane.

By the time war broke out, the situation had changed. There was great expansion in British production. In April 1916 it was announced that the Society of British Aircraft Constructors was being formed. Its object was to promote and protect the British aircraft industry. All the leading firms had

Sunbeam was another motor company trading on their production of aircraft engines during the war. They no doubt gave the impression that their engines were reliable.

joined and many others planned to join. The office of the society was to be at St Stephens House, Westminster.

In July 1917, Doctor Addison of the Ministry of Munitions, who since January had been responsible for the development of air industries, said that it was one of the ministry's biggest tasks. There were by this time 1,000 British factories in some way involved in the production of aircraft. The numbers of aircraft being produced had risen from 100 a month in May 1916 to 300 a month in May 1917.

There was increased secrecy about the production of aircraft as the war went on. In May 1914 Charles Grey, editor of *The Aeroplane*, found himself in court for publishing without authority the place of manufacture of aircraft. It seems that in the 3 and 10 April issues of the magazine an advertisement was published showing an image of an aircraft factory along with the address. Grey and the publishers were fined £50.

There was an interesting item in *The People's War Book* relating to aircraft manufacturing. The United States Signal Corps had compiled figures showing the materials needed to make an aircraft of an ordinary type, not including the engine:

Nails	4,326
Screws	3,337
Steel stampings	921
Forgings	798
Turnbuckles	276
Veneer – square feet	57
Wire – feet	3,262
Varnish – gallons	11
Dope – gallons	59
Aluminium – pounds	65
Rubber – feet	34
Linen – square yards	201
Spruce – feet	244
Pine – feet	58
Ash – feet	31
Hickory – feet	1½

As the war progressed the increased numbers of work places needed to produce aircraft began to be filled by women. In early 1917, Lord Derby

The Royal Aircraft Factory was the subject of a number of postcards during the war. This one shows a balloon above the works.

made an appeal at the Women's Meeting at the Albert Hall for help in the production of aircraft. The Woman's National Service was then inundated with applications.

Some of the jobs were of a skilled nature, such as for sand blasters and fitters' mates. The best recruits were women who were well educated. Willesden Polytechnic had begun to run carpentry courses for women who could then begin to work in the industry.

In May 1918 a report on the labour position in the munitions industry stated that until then there had been no regulation of wages for women. Because of the entry of so many women into the workplace it had been decided to set a minimum wage of five and a half pence an hour for girls under eighteen and at least six shillings a week for those over eighteen. This was the minimum wage for women in the workplace but in the aircraft industry women were to be paid at least sixpence an hour. This meant that they could earn much more than the minimum wage of six shillings a week. This was because women were doing jobs such as sheet metal work, which was usually done by men.

In April 1918, *The Illustrated War News* ran a series of articles on the women working on aircraft. According to the articles more aircraft were wanted on all fronts, and munitions factories all over the country had opened

es203 Farnborough; Royal Army Aircraft Factory.

Another view of the Royal Aircraft Factory, this one with an aeroplane above it.

additional departments to help produce these aircraft. The new departments were manned mainly by women who they said were adept at the work.

One factory in Birmingham was described as a large centre of specialized activities with highly trained artisans and workmen. The work at the factory was entirely suspended during the war and turned over to munitions. Then, later in the war, they began to produce aircraft. There were photographs of women at the factory painting the roundels on finished wings. There was also another photograph of a number of women sewing the covers on the wings of aircraft. The wings stood erect, with workers on both sides and at various heights.

Royal Balloon Factory and Royal Aircraft Factory

The origins of the Royal Balloon Factory date back to 1879 and an old shed at Woolwich Arsenal. It became the Army Balloon Equipment Store of the Royal Engineers. The factory moved to Chatham in 1882 and then to Aldershot in 1890, when it became Her Majesty's Balloon Factory. It also had a school of ballooning.

The balloons were used by the Army for observation and were tied to the ground. They were to gain fame for their use during the Boer War. Colonel Cody – a man who was to make his name in aviation – was producing man-lifting kites by 1904, which is also the year he went to work at the Balloon Factory.

The factory moved to Farnborough in 1905. Cody had by then begun to build kites with rudders and engines. The kites could be used when it was too windy for balloons. In 1907, the factory produced a large balloon with an engine and it flew over London with Cody as one of the pilots. Cody was then fired, as he was by this time more interested in aircraft and the factory wanted to concentrate on balloons.

In 1910, Geoffrey de Havilland met an old friend at the Olympia Exhibition. Fred Green worked at the Balloon Factory and told de Havilland that the factory was beginning to think about making aircraft. The factory then bought de Havilland's aircraft and gave him a job.

By 1911, those involved with balloons had moved on and the factory became the Royal Aircraft Factory. De Havilland stayed there until the war began. He then joined the RFC and was sent to fly aircraft off the coast of Scotland, watching for U-boats. It soon became clear that he was of more use in design and he went to work for Airco.

De Havilland was responsible for designing the first aircraft built at the factory, the BE1, which first flew at the end of 1911. This was followed by the BE2 in early 1912. This was similar to the first aircraft but with a better engine. It was followed later that year by the BE3.

The BE2 was a superior aircraft to many of those that took part in the Larkhill Military Aircraft Competition in 1912 but it wasn't eligible to enter as one of the judges worked at the Aircraft Factory. Despite this, the government ordered the BE2a, which was also made at other factories such as the Coventry Ordnance Works and Handley Page. This was followed by the BE2b. The aircraft was to undergo several new developments during the war.

There were several reports in the national press of problems at the factory during the war. One criticism was the retention of male workers of military age. A special meeting of the Farnborough Tribunal, which decided on whether men should serve in the war, took place at the town hall. The chairman was Mr G.W. Collins and the recruiting officer was Captain J.R. Croxford. They had received a letter from the factory stating that, since September 1916, 473 men of military age had been discharged from the factory. Captain Croxford said that he doubted if many of those men were in the Army. The chairman also said that there were 200 young men employed as draughtsmen in the factory who would be rendering better service in the Army.

Early in 1916 there was a report carried out on the Royal Aircraft Factory by the Army Council on the direction of the War Office to find out if the factory was being run efficiently. They listed the function of the factory as: 'The original design of aeroplanes and engines, improvement of existing designs, manufacture of experimental aeroplanes, engines and their parts. The production of aeroplanes in limited quantities.'

They stated that as the War Office said that the Royal Aircraft Factory should be devoted to experimental rather than manufacturing purposes it could not be considered to be working on commercial lines. It was described as a large experimental facility where expenses must therefore be high. They did, however, state that the production of engine spare parts for aircraft should be economic.

The report found that the factory spent twenty-two per cent of its time on experimental work, thirty-five per cent on aircraft production, thirty-three per cent on repairs and production of spare parts, and ten per cent on repairs to engines and production of engines spare parts. The design of a new aeroplane took from six to nine months before production in any numbers could commence.

Due to the pressure of the war it was often necessary to put out orders to other companies for aircraft before the design was complete. This often led to alterations to aircraft produced and it was often part of the contract that they would have to be altered, and in some cases scrap the parts affected. This led to compensation being paid to the companies producing the machines.

The report went on to state that the salary paid to the designers at the factory was low and unlikely to attract highly skilled persons. It then went on to say that the number of people employed in the non-productive areas of the factory, such as stores, was higher than normal in other government establishments.

They also found that the aircraft being produced were often not up to standard due to them having less powerful engines than those available in the private sector. The more powerful engines were being supplied to the factory, but the numbers needed to increase.

There were even doubts as to the exact aims of the factory and, in July 1916, a report from the president of the Air Board, The Earl Curzon of Kedleston, expressed this doubt to the War Committee. It first commented upon the report of the committee appointed by the Army Council. This

Women did a number of jobs producing aircraft. The women in this photograph are acting as joiners' mates producing seaplane floats.

investigated the management and organization of the factory. The Air Board disagreed with some of the Army Council findings.

The Army report had stated that thirty-five per cent of the factory time was devoted to the production of aircraft. The Air Board, however, found that this time was spent in new experimental construction, not the production of aircraft. They found that only ten per cent of factory time was spent in producing aircraft. The Air Board also disagreed with the Army report's suggestion to place the factory under a board of management, which may have been suitable for a private concern but not for a military organization.

The Air Board thought that appointing a head of the design branch and a head of production would be a better way to proceed. Overall control of the factory could be overseen by the Department of Military Aeronautics at the War Office. Although the Air Board thought that an increase in the production of aircraft was desirable on a financial basis, it should not hamper the experimental aims of the factory.

Short Brothers

The Short brothers were making balloons from the turn of the century. In 1903 they were renting two railway arches in Battersea and won an Army balloon contract in 1905. In 1908, they met with the Wright brothers and agreed to produce six of the Wright Fliers, which were all bought by members of the Aero Club of Great Britain.

In 1909, Frank McClean of the Aero Club bought a site at the shell beach at Shellness, near what was known as Mussell Manor, close to Leysdown on the Isle of Sheppey. The club opened a flying ground there and the Short brothers opened their aircraft factory nearby.

The Shellness site did not last long and both the now 'Royal' Aero Club and the Short Brothers company moved to a site at Eastchurch, also on Sheppey, in 1910. In 1911, Short Brothers built the first twin-engine aircraft, the S.39.

In August 1912, an article appeared in *The Manchester Guardian* stating that Mr Horace Short, builder of naval hydroplanes in Sheppey, said that owing to the scarcity of housing accommodation at Eastchurch, the firm would have to move their factory to another part of the country.

The factory had outgrown the home of the aeroplane. Eastchurch, once seen as a future centre of industry, had lost its opportunity. Short said that he could employ another 300 men at once but could not do so as there was nowhere near the factory where they could live. Eastchurch village was overcrowded and the cost of living in the area was very expensive. The company had no assistance from local people and public lighting, water and sanitation were almost non-existent in the area.

Women also trained as lathe operators. Here they are turning aero engine cylinders.

Short Brothers did not move very far – only to Rochester, in 1913. In September 1914, the government invited companies to design a long-range seaplane. The Short 184 was similar to the seaplane they had entered in the Circuit of Britain race the previous year. The order from the government for the seaplanes was so large that they had to be produced by other factories as well. A land plane version of the 184 was later produced as a bomber. They were mainly overtaken, however, by the more popular Handley Page 0/100.

Howard T. Wright

Howard T. Wright began to make aircraft in 1907. He rented two railway arches in Battersea next to Short Brothers' premises at a time when the company was making balloons. In 1908 Wright had an order for a biplane that he showed at Olympia in 1909. It was then tested at a field at Fambridge, in Essex.

In 1909 he built at least three biplanes and tried to introduce mass production techniques. This meant that when an aircraft was ordered it could be delivered within two weeks. In 1910, Wright built a Farman type biplane with a Gnome engine. It was used by Thomas Sopwith for his early flights. In 1911 the company was taken over by Coventry Ordnance Works and Wright went to work for them.

Colonel Cody

Samuel Franklin Cowdery, who was later known as Colonel Cody, had already been involved with making kites and balloons at the Royal Balloon Factory but began to make aircraft in 1907. By September 1908, he had managed to get his aircraft off the ground but described it as a jump rather than flying. In October, however, he managed to fly at a height of 20 feet for twenty-seven seconds and travelled more than 1,300 feet. Then the aircraft crashed. Cody has since been credited as the first man to fly in England.

Cody carried on working on his aircraft and added new engines and seats for passengers. He agreed to fly at the Doncaster Air Show in 1909. He arrived at the meeting as an American and was greeted by a band who were playing the *Star Spangled Banner* and displaying an American flag. He then became a British citizen and *God Save the Queen* was played while the American flag was replaced with the Union flag. A number of the British aviation prizes of the time were only open to British citizens.

Albert Verdon Roe – Avro

Albert Verdon Roe claimed to have flown at Brooklands in 1908, but this was not officially recognized.

Roe then went to work in two railway arches at Lea Marshes in East London. Large crowds would gather to watch him try to fly. Leyton Council then made a charge of being a public nuisance against him so he would fly early in the morning before the men from the council were around. The council finally served a summons on Roe one morning as he sat in his aircraft, which had just crashed.

After moving to other sites in London, Roe moved to Manchester in 1910 and formed Avro. A number of aircraft were built there and a flying school was opened. In 1912, they built the world's first aircraft with an enclosed cockpit.

The Avro 504 was ordered by the War Office in early 1914. The 504D, which was also used by the flying services, was a two-seater. Some of the aircraft were used as bombers. The 504As were also built by other companies to fulfil the orders from the War Department. They also built a seaplane, the Avro 510.

Some occupations in the aircraft industry were what were seen as 'women's work'. These women are sewing aircraft coverings.

Avro was one of the companies to suffer from labour strikes during the war. A report by Winston Churchill, 'In the Munitions Industries' of May 1918, stated that at the Manchester works 1,532 employees lost 3,064 work days through strikes.

Handley Page

There seems to be some dispute over which was the first company to make aircraft in Britain. Some say it was Shorts, others claim that it was Handley Page. There were obviously others making aircraft before Handley Page but their claim seems to be that when they opened the factory at Barking Creek in 1909, theirs were the first buildings to be used exclusively to make aircraft. The buildings were the aircraft sheds from the Dagenham flying ground, which had been dismantled and moved to Barking Creek after the Dagenham site closed.

The first thing they made there was a glider. There was a large mound within the grounds that was used to launch the aircraft. It was then tested on the marshes lining the Thames. Then a powered aircraft was made, the HP1, or the Bluebird, which was not a success. They also made a Baden Powell Scout and a Mackenzie Hughes triplane.

The biggest early success was the EHP5, made in 1911. It was a two-seater plane with a Gnome engine and was the first aircraft to fly over London. In 1912 the company needed to expand and moved to bigger premises in Cricklewood.

The first military aircraft produced by Handley Page was the 0/100 heavy bomber. It came about as a means of reprisal against German bombing by Zeppelin. It was a very large aircraft with twin engines. It began to be used in late 1916 by the RNAS. This was followed by the updated 0/400. A number of these were built in America under licence.

In a report to the government in September 1917 it was stated that additional facilities for the manufacture of Handley Page aircraft would be provided to enable the company to produce an extra 100 machines a month, which was the maximum they thought they would be capable of. It was hoped that the company would produce 200 aircraft a month by the middle of 1918.

On 24 September 1918 there was a report in *The Times* on a visit to the Handley Page works by foreign journalists. They were shown the factory buildings, where thousands of people, mainly women, were working.

They were taken through various sheds where huge bombers were waiting to be launched. There were also smaller aircraft that were destined to protect the bombers. Outside on the landing field some aircraft had bodies of 50 feet in length that could carry eight to ten crewmembers.

The journalists were then given a flight over London at a height of 2,000 feet in one of the bombers that would, it was stated, one day awaken the population of Berlin to the supremacy of our air force.

At lunch it was mentioned that it had only been ten years since the first exhibition of flying in Europe by the Wright brothers in which aircraft had a weight limit of around 9 stone. Now, three and a half tons was nothing to an aircraft. One Handley Page machine had already carried twenty-one passengers and a pilot.

Humber Ltd.

The firm of Humber Ltd. of Coventry was reported to be making fifty Blériot type aircraft in September 1909. Mr Ballin Hinde, one of the founders of the Midland Aero Club, had joined the directors of the company. He was confident that there would be a demand for the aircraft in England and abroad. He believed that the industry was beyond the pastime stage. The machines were to go on sale for £400 each and the company was trying to obtain land near the factory for testing the machines.

Flight Magazine mentioned the production of the Blériot aircraft in their 25 September 1909 issue. They claimed that Coventry, where Humber was based, would be the first town in Great Britain to seriously take up the manufacture of aeroplanes. They were also planning to produce Voisin and Farman machines at the works.

The Farman production was based on an agreement that Henri Farman would give exhibitions of flying in his aircraft in Coventry.

The British and Colonial Aeroplane Company

The British and Colonial Aeroplane Company opened in February 1910. The man behind its opening was Sir George White, chairman of the Bristol Tramway and Carriage Company. The company began with an advantage over many other early aviation manufacturers in that it was well funded. It was based at Filton and also opened flying schools at Brooklands and Larkhill.

Filton : :
Works : :
Committee.

1918.

Peace on earth, goodwill
towards men.

There were numerous union problems in aircraft production during the war. This was the cover of a 1918 booklet for the Filton Works Committee.

The company began with a British-made version of a French aircraft designed by Gabriel Voisin. It was not a success and failed to fly, despite several adaptations, and they eventually received compensation from the French manufacturers.

New plans were drawn up for a design by Henri Farman by George Challenger. Twenty of these, the Bristol Boxkite, were made to provide aircraft for the flying schools. More than seventy were eventually built.

Challenger left and was replaced by Frank Barnwell, who worked on designs for naval aircraft. By the beginning of the war the company employed 200 workers. Demand for the new Bristol Scout led to the opening of a new factory at Brislington, near Bristol. The company eventually developed the F2.B Bristol Fighter, one of the successful aircraft of the war, and it continued to be successful after the war ended.

They also produced a reliable monoplane, the Bristol Monoplane Scout. Popular with pilots, it suffered from the War Office prejudice against monoplanes and only just over a 100 were built.

A series of cartoons from the Filton Works Committee booklet. The characters at each top corner are L.T. Taylor, secretary, and T.J. Scottow, chairman.

By the end of the war the company employed more than 3,000 people at its two factories. It then changed its name to the Bristol Aeroplane Company Limited. Unlike other aviation companies that closed after the war, Bristol continued to produce aircraft for the RAF.

Grahame-White Aviation Company

Grahame-White had been well known in aviation before he opened his company in 1911. He also opened a flying school at Hendon, which became Hendon Aerodrome. At first, the company produced aircraft of their own design. When the war began they also produced Morane Sauliniers under licence.

In January 1915, *Flight Magazine* published an illustrated article on the Grahame-White Company. The article stated that the company held a unique position in the aviation industry. Not only were the aeroplanes designed and constructed at the works at Hendon, but pupils were instructed in flying at the London Aerodrome.

In June 1917, King George V and Princess Mary visited the factory. The large workforce gave the royal couple a great reception. They spoke to the workers in the plane assembling shop and also visited the seaplane department.

The doping room was manned by a female workforce. The process carried out here involved doping the material that covered the aircrafts' rudders and ailerons. The dope gave off dangerous fumes so the workshop had large fans to remove the bad air.

The neatness of the finish of British aircraft was credited to the skills of the girls working in aircraft production. An advertisement for the company published during the war claimed that the factories contained the newest and best in organization and machinery and a skilled designing staff that was continuously employed. The advertisement also listed the Grahame-White School of Flying – the first British flying school. It was world renowned and the London Aerodrome was the most perfectly equipped flying ground in the world.

Aeroplane Supply Company

In 1911, Holt Thomas secured the British rights to manufacture Farman machines using Gnome and Le Rhone engines. He obtained premises at

Women doping the wings of aircraft.

Hendon and formed the Aeroplane Supply Company. In April 1912, the company was known by the name Airco and entered a Farman aircraft for the government trials at Larkhill. The aircraft was a SE7, or the Longhorn.

One of the most famous names in aviation, Geoffrey de Havilland, began his aircraft manufacturing career with Frank Hearle at Fulham in 1908. He tested his aircraft at Eastchurch, but only made two. He sold the second aircraft to the Royal Balloon Factory and then went to work there in 1911.

De Havilland later went to work with Holt Thomas at the Aircraft Company Limited. Although de Havilland was called up when war began, it was clear that he was more valuable in designing aircraft and he returned to work for Holt Thomas.

Geoffrey de Havilland came back to work at the company in 1914 and by the following year, they were employing 600 people. They made the aircraft types DH1 through to DH5 during the war. Some of these aircraft were subcontracted to Savages of King's Lynn. By the end of hostilities they employed more than 4,000 and were the largest aircraft company in the world.

One of the companies that produced parts for Airco was Peter Hooker Ltd. of Walthamstow, in North East London. They produced Gnome and Le Rhone engines under licence and were one of the first companies to use Y alloy, which was a type of aluminium alloy for pistons. The company covered 26 acres and employed 1,500 workers.

In a report from the Air Board in March 1917, labour difficulties were mentioned in the aircraft manufacturing establishments in the London area. This was reported to have culminated at the important works of Messrs Peter Hooker. The Controller of Aeronautical Supplies informed the board that there were signs of a strongly seditious and syndicalist element at the works. They thought that strong action needed to be taken by the government, which may lead to a strike. The question of what action to take was one for the Ministry of Munitions but also concerned the board as it may have temporarily affected the output of aircraft.

There seems to have been some other problems with the companies supplying Airco, as in February 1918 there was trouble at the Integral Propeller Company at Hendon, which supplied propellers for many of the machines used by the flying services. According to a report from the Ministry of Labour, the workers were in revolt. This was mainly due to the difficulties of getting enough food. There was a serious belief that starvation could be a possibility before the end of the year.

The company had been producing 190 aircraft a month and built their own village, Roe Green, for their workers to live in. It was then sold to Birmingham Small Arms Company in 1919. They had no interest in aviation but the following year, the de Havilland Aircraft Company was formed.

Coventry Ordnance Works

The Coventry Ordnance Works had been formed in 1905 by a consortium of British shipbuilders to produce naval guns. The company took over the Howard T. Wright Company in Battersea in 1911 and used the site to make their aircraft.

A competition to find planes for the Royal Flying Corps was held at Larkhill in 1912. The company had Howard Wright design two biplanes for the competition. They were both two-seaters, one side by side, the other tandem. The side by side plane had a Gnome engine. The planes were built at Battersea and tested at Brooklands by Thomas Sopwith, who had been employed as test pilot. On one occasion, the aircraft carried three passengers. Two of them sat on the wings outside the cockpit.

One of the aircraft didn't reach Larkhill in time for the competition. The other would not start on the day of its intended flight.

There were reports of aircraft that were needed at the front being delayed by industrial action in some factories. One of these was at the Coventry factory in November 1917. It was reported in *The Times* that aircraft workers were standing idle due to the dispute. The company was one of those to become part of English Electric in 1918.

Blériot Manufacturing Company

Louis Blériot was making aircraft in France as early as 1907. His aircraft continued to develop and in July 1909 he became the first man to fly across the English Channel. He then went on to form flying schools at Brooklands and Hendon while still producing aircraft in France. In 1915, he decided that the British Government would be more likely to buy aircraft that were made in Britain. This must have been a change from the government's earlier views.

He opened the Blériot Manufacturing Aircraft Company in 1915, but the Blériot was already seen as out of date and there were few orders. Blériot did, however, produce aircraft for some other manufacturers. There was an attempt to sell shares in the company in June 1915. An advertisement appeared in *The Times* with the headline 'Your country needs more aircraft'. The treasury had sanctioned the issue of 100,000 £1 shares. It didn't make any difference and by July 1916 the company was wound up and Blériot opened a new company, Blériot & Spad, in Addlestone in Surrey. After the war, in 1919 the company changed its name to the Air Navigation & Engineering Company.

Sopwith Aviation Company

The Sopwith Company was formed at the end of 1912, after Thomas Sopwith had been involved in flying and other companies for some time. The

A group of women aircraft workers with one of their aircraft in the background. For some reason the photograph has been cut in half.

first premises were at Kingston upon Thames, in an old roller-skating rink in Canbury Park Road. The company later opened a factory in Woolstan, Hampshire.

The first aircraft produced was a Bat Boat, a flying boat that could also be used on land. The company came into its own during the war. They employed thousands of people and produced more than 16,000 aircraft, although many of these were subcontracted to other companies.

There were a number of aircraft types produced in the war, such as the Sopwith Baby, mainly used by the RNAS. The 9901 was better known as the 1½ Strutter. It was the first British-designed two-seater tractor fighter – an aircraft with a propeller at the front that pulled it rather than a 'pusher', which had the propeller at the rear. There was also the Sopwith Pup. Both these aircraft were the first successful tractor fighters in Britain that could fire a gun through the propeller.

The aircraft produced by the Sopwith Company went to the RNAS as the company had exclusive contracts with the Admiralty. The fact that the RFC could not get supplies of the aircraft showed the problems in having two separate air services. The RFC finally began to get Sopwith aircraft, but from Ruston, Proctor and Vickers, as many Sopwith aircraft were subcontracted

A postcard showing the Lord Mayor of London addressing the staff of Whitehead Aircraft Factory.

to other manufacturers. Some of the 1½ Strutters were transferred from the RNAS to the RFC in time for the Somme offensive.

The Sopwith Triplane was a successful fighter but was used by very few apart from a few RNAS squadrons. It is thought that this led to the development of a number of three-winged aircraft, the most successful being the Fokker – well known for its use by Baron von Richthofen, more widely known as the Red Baron.

The best known and most successful Sopwith was the Camel, which was responsible for more kills than any other type of British fighter. It was also used by the Americans and the Belgians. The company made more than 5,000 of them. As with other companies producing successful aircraft, the production of Sopwith planes was often subcontracted to other producers.

Towards the end of the war Sopwith produced a number of aircraft named after animals, none of which became well known. Cecil Lewis, in his book *Sagittarius Rising*, mentions visiting the Sopwith works in 1918. He said that Camels were being produced in their hundreds. He also saw an experimental two-seater fighter called a Hippo and a new triplane with six guns. Both were cancelled when the war ended.

Whitehead Aircraft Company Ltd.

John Alexander Whitehead was born in England but had been living in America. He later returned to England. It seems that Whitehead was a carpenter who had worked on aircraft. He founded the Whitehead Aircraft Company in 1915 in Richmond, Surrey. He approached the War Office, who gave him a contract to build six BE2bs.

The first contract must have been a success as Whitehead was then given a further contract for 100 Maurice Farman MF.11 Shorthorns. This led to expansion of the company and Whitehead bought Hanworth Park in South West London, and more land to the north-west of the park at Feltham. He used this land to build a larger factory. Hanworth Park was also known as the London Air Park and was a grass airfield. The airfield became an Aircraft Acceptance Park. This was where the aircraft were tested before being accepted by the RFC.

Whitehead also had an order from Sopwith to build Sopwith Pups. The Pups were flown from the airfield to be tested before delivery. In a company advertisement in *The Aeroplane* magazine they were called Whiteheads Fighting Scouts. There was a plane built by Whitehead called the Comet, which does not seem to have been used. There was also a seaplane that never went into production.

By 1916, the company employed more than 600 workers. There was also a flying school, which began in 1917. The company became Whitehead Aviation Construction Company Ltd. and later, Whitehead Aircraft Ltd.

Whitehead had grand plans for what he wanted to do and had German prisoners of war working to cover the river that flowed through the airfield and have it run underground. The work was reported in *The Times* on 17 October 1917. The report stated that Hanworth Park was an ideal airfield

Petrol's Part in the Great War.—No. VII.

AIRCRAFT'S SPLENDID AID

THE Allies, between them, have 1,250 aeroplanes and seaplanes. Germany and Austria together possess some 600, or only half the Allied strength. We have it on no less an authority than that of General French himself that the British aviators have established a personal ascendency over the enemy's airmen. Proof of which is to be seen in the frequent daring and successful air-raids by our magnificent Flying Corps.

Both War Office and Admiralty are using

PRATT'S
Motor Spirit

for operations at the Front. Pratt's enjoys also the full confidence of our Allies, who are using it in enormous quantities.

By Appointment.

Anglo-American Oil Co., Ltd.   *36, Queen Anne's Gate, London, S.W.*

According to this advertisement for Pratt's Motor Spirit, the Allies have 1,250 aeroplanes, whilst the enemy has only 600. This was supposedly on the word of General French. The advert was published in November 1914.

apart from the Cardinal Wolsey, better known as the Longford River, which ran across it. The stream was about 10 feet wide and needed a conduit capable of passing 27,000,000 gallons of water daily. The construction took months and was large enough for fifty soldiers to march through it. It also took tons of concrete to complete it.

The Lord Mayor of London threw a switch that diverted the river through the tunnel. He then made a speech congratulating Mr Whitehead and the progress made by his company in the production of aircraft. The mayor also praised the unique character of the undertaking he had witnessed.

Whitehead hoped that the area would eventually become a London peacetime airport. He treated his workers well and provided them with a large canteen and leisure activities that included a football team that played other aircraft producers' teams.

Unfortunately it seems that Whitehead's grand plans outstripped the production of aircraft. Although they did get other contracts after the Sopwith contract ended in 1918, the company eventually closed in 1919.

May, Harden & May Ltd.

May, Harden & May were based on Southampton Water at Hythe in Kent. They were manufacturing flying boats. When Airco got a contract for twenty-five Felixstowe F2A flying boats in 1917, they subcontracted them to May, Harden & May. They were delivered by September 1918. The aircraft had been redesigned by Commander John Porte from Felixstowe.

Chapter 3

The War at Home

Nineteen-fourteen

The progress in the design of aircraft had been rapid since the early days at Dagenham. The international events on the horizon had an even greater effect on the development of the machines than a normal interest in flying could ever have done. There was, however, still a severe shortage of aircraft for military use at the outbreak of war and private aircraft were requisitioned. There would not have been much point in private owners keeping their aircraft as all flying, apart from that carried out by the services, was banned over Britain.

The responsibility for home defence from German bombing was given to the Royal Navy Air Service. This was because the Royal Flying Corps was far from ready to take the responsibility. Churchill argued that neither were the RNAS with what resources they had at the time. The RNAS had only ninety aircraft and not all of these were serviceable; of those that were, some had already gone to France.

Even anti-aircraft guns and searchlights were in short supply. In September there were only thirty-three AA guns available for the country's defence. They were manned by the Royal Navy Volunteer Reserves Anti Aircraft Corps.

Bombing from aeroplanes was still not common at the beginning of the war. The US Army had dropped bombs from aircraft as early as 1910 as a practice but it was the Italians who first used bombs in real action in 1911. So, bombers were actually in existence before fighter planes, although the bombs used were usually adapted artillery shells or grenades.

The first bombers of the war were probably French Voisins. They had a two-man crew and could carry more than 130lbs of bombs. The Voisins were updated throughout the war. The Russians had the first four-engined aircraft; the Ilya Mourometz, designed by Sikorsky. It flew from 1913, could carry more than 2,000lb of bombs and was used on the Eastern Front.

The Germans also wanted to develop a long-range bomber that would reach London. They had already bombed Belgium in August, including an attempt to bomb the Belgian queen, Queen Elizabeth, and her children in the Royal Palace in Brussels. They also bombed Paris from as early as August 1914. However, most of the early attacks on England came from the sea rather than from the air. In November, Yarmouth was shelled, but most of the shells fell short or did not go off. There were no planes in action at the time from the airbase in the town.

Early in the war the RNAS only had a few balloons. These were needed to watch out for submarines, as aircraft could not spend long periods over the sea. One of the pilots of these early balloons was T. Williams. He tested semi and rigid airships. Fifty small balloons, known as Sea Scouts or Sub Searchers, were ordered. The crews trained at Kingsnorth Airship Station on the Isle of Grain. The crew would spend eight to ten hours over the sea in open cockpits. The pilot would be responsible for dropping bombs on any submarines they spotted. The early balloons were only armed with a pistol, apart from the bombs, but later they had Lewis Guns.

The RNAS aircraft from Yarmouth carried bombs from early in the war. Landing with the bombs still on board could be dangerous so they were normally dropped at sea before the aircraft came in to land if they had not been used on the enemy. This was not always safe either, as when Lieutenant Lan-Davies came in to land he dropped his bombs and the resulting explosion blew the tail off his aircraft. The pilot was knocked unconscious and the observer, P. Hendrey, fell out. Hendrey then managed to save the unconscious pilot.

As the war progressed there was still a severe shortage of aircraft and of vital parts. Engines still mainly came from France until Daimler was allowed to build Gnome engines under licence in Britain. Parts were even scarcer. Up until the war magnetos had been mainly imported from Germany and were in short supply, as were spark plugs, as very few of these were made in Britain.

The ferries that ran out of Harwich to the Continent often carried wounded men back from the Continent as passengers. One man who had an unusual role in the air was Sergeant W. Knight, who was in the St John's Ambulance Brigade. We know from his papers that are now in the Imperial War Museum that he worked on the SS *St Petersburg* between Harwich and Flushing caring for the wounded being brought back to England. He was a member of the Royal Navy Sick Berth Reserve. When kite balloons

GERMAN INCENDIARY BOMB WEIGHT ABOUT 16 LLs.
DROPPED AT MALDON DURING AIR RAID. APRIL 16/15.   F.H.

A German incendiary bomb dropped on Maldon in Essex in June 1915.

were developed to be fitted to warships to watch for submarines, Knight volunteered as an observer on the kites. He then became a member of the RNAS. He was trained at Roehampton, where army balloon observers were also trained.

In December 1914 a warning was given to civilians in London. This was not only against the danger from enemy bombs but also from the shrapnel from the anti-aircraft guns used to try and shoot them down. The public were warned to keep under cover when hearing gunfire.

The officer commanding the Portsmouth defences said that in the case of bombs being dropped, any pieces collected by the public should be handed in to the police so they could be passed on to the military. This was so that they would know the size and type of bombs being dropped.

The first air raids occurred in December and were carried out by aircraft rather than airship. Two aircraft bombed Dover and Erith on 24th and 25th of the month; three bombs were dropped but there were no casualties.

The need for more airfields was obvious, especially in the south-east, which was where the enemy airships were expected to arrive when they eventually attacked. There was already a base at the Isle of Grain. New RNAS bases were quickly opened at Clacton-on-Sea, Hainault Farm, Chingford and Burnham-on-Crouch. The Clacton base had an unusual headquarters building – the West Beach Napoleonic Martello Tower.

There was an immediate blackout enforced in London, which was not popular with the inhabitants as there had been no air raids there so far in 1914. Airship raids came soon after the first aircraft attack but occurred in other parts of the country.

Nineteen-fifteen

Three German airships set out on 19 January. They were the *L3*, *L4* and *L6*. The *L6* had engine trouble and went back, while the *L3* dropped nine bombs near Yarmouth; an elderly couple were killed. The *L4* dropped bombs near Cromer, Sheringham, Hunstanton and King's Lynn, killing a man and woman and injuring thirteen others. After this some car-mounted lights and machine guns were sent to East Anglia, as most anti-aircraft equipment was based around London even though no raids had yet reached the capital.

When the raid took place that led to the two deaths in Yarmouth, it was at first unclear whether this attack had been from an airship or an aeroplane. Eventually, one of the unexploded bombs that was found was said to be too large to have come from an aeroplane. The following month, posters were widely distributed showing which aircraft were British and which were enemy craft.

The early attacks were to lead to a surge in the building of new airfields. Twenty were opened in Essex alone in the next two years. Some of these were landing grounds rather than airfields and had a small force of men

Southend was often a target for the enemy as it was one of the places where they crossed the coast. This raid was in West Road, Prittlewell.

to light torches for night landing. Some of the earlier RNAS fields were taken over by the RFC. In April 1915 they took over Hainault Farm but then opened a new RNAS base less than a mile away at Fairlop. It was the site that had been used as an experimental airfield by Handley Page while working at Barking. Burnham-on-Crouch was also taken over by the RFC in April. Goldhanger had hardly been used by the RNAS when it was taken over by the RFC in August.

By April, when the RFC had acquired new airfields, Home Defence units had also been completely reorganized. There were several Home Defence squadrons based in Essex. No. 39 Squadron was the first and had three flights, based at Hainault Farm, North Weald and Suttons Farm, Hornchurch. They all had BE2cs. Squadron No. 37 had been based at Orford Ness but by September it also had three flights, based at Rochford, Stow Maries and Goldhanger. They were equipped with a mixture of BE2cs and BE12s

One of the pilots who was to become famous throughout the country was based at Hornchurch. He had begun his military career by entering Sandhurst when the war began. In December 1914, William Leefe Robinson had joined the Worcester Regiment as a second lieutenant and was posted

Orford Ness was used as an experimental area. Being an island, the public were kept away. The photograph shows the remains of a First World War hangar. The island has only recently been open to the public again.

to Cornwall. He found the posting boring and decided on a more exciting military career by transferring to the RFC in March. Robinson was then sent to France as an observer.

Some of those in charge of the new air services were stuck in the past, as observer L. Howden experienced. Again, from his papers, which are now in the Imperial War Museum, he remembered that the old generals in charge thought that flying needed similar skills to those of horse riding. They thought of airmen as the cavalry of the air. Therefore the first part of the training for observers was to learn how to ride a horse. They then had to learn how to fire both Lewis and Vickers machine guns. Howden was based at Farnborough, where he had to ride on a railway truck on a bending track and fire the guns as the truck twisted and turned. He then went to the Regent Street Polytechnic to learn Morse code for signalling.

The enlistment of officers was another matter. When the future Wing Commander Wilkins applied for a commission in the RNAS in February, he had references from a Captain Whitely of the 23rd Battalion the London Regiment. It stated that he had known Wilkins since he was a boy and he was an excellent athlete and quite fearless. The training he had received at

Lieutenant William Leefe Robinson VC rose to fame when he shot down the first airship over land in England.

Hailbury College would ensure this. Public school boys were considered to make the best officers.

Wilkins also had another reference from a solicitor named Young Hyland, who described him as upright and honourable in character. He was said to have had courage and endurance, judgement and obedience. I'm not sure how a solicitor would know this about someone but it seemed to work, as Wilkins got his commission.

Further raids took place in April when the airships *L5* and *L6* bombed areas around the coast. The *L5* bombed Lowestoft and Southwold and the

L6 bombed Maldon and Heybridge. Several aircraft took off but could not find the airships. This was to be a common problem during raids.

To stop the airships coming, there were attempts to bomb the airship sheds on the Continent in April. First the RFC tried, and then RNAS, but neither raid was very successful.

German Zeppelins were by now carrying out frequent bombing raids across the south-east. A guard at Romford Railway Station reported a Zeppelin that was visible for more than half an hour in May 1915. Nearby Southend was bombed on the 10th. It was estimated that 100 bombs were dropped, but there was only one death – a woman who was a member of the Salvation Army. There was extensive damage, however, and houses in West Street were damaged by incendiaries. A timber yard was also damaged as well as a number of other buildings.

It was the last night of May when London was finally bombed. The Zeppelins then continued to bomb several other parts of the country for the rest of 1915. The early military warplanes and their weapons had little effect on the German airships until new ammunition was invented.

The German airships did not survive totally unscathed. In June, Flight Lieutenant R. Warneford was returning from a bombing raid on airship sheds at Agathe when he spotted the *LZ37* near Ostende. He was flying a

"SPOTTED."
THE ZEPP RAIDER.
Passed for publication, by Press Bureau

This old postcard shows how airships could be caught in the beams of searchlights. Early in the war the lights were in very short supply.

Morane Parasol monoplane. He bombed the airship until it burst into flames. The combined effects of the explosion of the airship and engine trouble led to his having to land in enemy territory. Warneford then managed to repair his aircraft and flew home. He was awarded the Victoria Cross but then died ten days later.

Having returned from France where he had been wounded, William Leefe Robinson went to Farnborough in June 1915 to learn to fly. He was flying solo by July and qualified within two weeks. He then went to the Central Flying School at Upavon before being posted to Castle Bromwich, where his job was to deliver aircraft. Robinson would often land somewhere on the way to deliver new machines and wherever he did so he was treated like a celebrity just because he was a pilot.

The future Wing Commander Wilkins RNAS had been commissioned in February, and by June he was based at Eastchurch. He wrote to his father saying that he would not be coming up to London for at least a week as he was going to fly as many aircraft as possible. The school was shut to all pilots apart from Wilkins and one other so they could have all the flying they wanted.

The memorial in the village of Eastchurch shows a number of the early aircraft that flew there.

An interesting old postcard of London during the First World War. Despite the searchlights, because a raid is in progress, there are still people on the streets.

Wilkins went on to list the aircraft at Eastchurch. There were Maurice Farmans, Shorts, Avros, Bristols, Thompsons, Sopwiths and a Blériot monoplane. More pilots must have arrived, as he went on to say that there had been three crashes in the last forty-eight hours and one pilot had been killed.

Wilkins described how he had flown over Sheerness and when he got back he was told that firing had been heard at the aerodrome. There were bullet holes in his wings. As he had no British markings on the aircraft, he had been fired on by the defences at Sheerness but had not even heard the gunfire.

There were often reports of pilots arriving at the front with few hours' experience of solo flying. When Lieutenant C. Young began training at Northolt, however, he seemed to take things gradually. According to his log book, as a member of No. 20 training squad he began flying on 10 May but did not fly solo until 6 June. The flying consisted mainly of circuits of the aerodrome, landing and taking off. He later went on to fire his guns and passed out as a pilot in August.

One of the most serious raids so far took place in June, when Hull was bombed. There were twenty-four deaths and fifty injured. The ineffective action taken against airships until this time made it seem as though the only way to stop them was for pilots to ram them – that was if they could find them. The airships were easily lost in the clouds and although their engines could often be heard from the ground, the sound of the aircrafts' own engines drowned out the airship engines from the pilots when they were airborne.

On 9-10 August, a large group of airships bombed a number of different parts of the country, killing seventeen and injuring twenty-one. There was some success against the enemy when the *L12* was severely damaged by AA fire and came down in the sea. It was towed into Ostende but was damaged beyond repair by fire. The airships came again in August and September.

The pilots had by this time another weapon for use against the airships. Ranken darts had been invented by Francis Ranken RN. They were incendiary weapons but had to be used from above the airships. Once again, the problem was that the pilots could often still not see the airships, unless they were caught in the beams of searchlights or being fired upon by AA guns. Of course, many of the areas being attacked still had very few lights or guns.

Harold Hillier was a member of the 23rd Reserve Squadron RFC. When he was posted to another squadron his transfer card contained details of

A German incendiary bomb that was dropped on London. It was bound in tarred rope with an explosive charge to set it off.

A German propaganda card showing the *King Stephen* trawler leaving an airship crew to drown. The captain feared the Germans would overpower his smaller crew if they picked them up.

his training in artillery co-operation, bomb sighting, machine gun use and aerial fighting. He had flown five hours solo in a Maurice Farman and had graduated in September.

There was a raid on London on the night of 13 October, when there were 127 deaths and injuries, almost entirely civilian. The raids occurred in five different parts of London and the surrounding area. There seemed to be no tactical purpose for the attacks as in many cases the crews of the Zeppelins seemed to have little idea of where or what they were bombing.

Photographs of many of the damaged buildings appeared in publications such as *The Illustrated War News*. The locations of the damage were not given, however, as this may have helped the German raiders in pinpointing where they had bombed.

By the end of 1915, Leefe Robinson had been posted to Farningham in Kent, on loan to No. 10 Reserve Squadron Home Defence Unit. There were only twenty aircraft to defend London from raids and the pilots were chosen because of their ability to fly at night, when the raids took place.

The year had not been a success for the men defending the country from air raids. There had been twenty raids, with 207 deaths and 533 injuries suffered. There was little success against the raiders, who seemed to be immune to attack.

The arrival of Zeppelins bombing the country had an effect on the highest powers in the land. The Directorate of Military Aeronautics at the War Office was situated in a loft at the top of the building. It became known as Zeppelin Terrace.

Nineteen-sixteen

Airship raids continued into 1916 and at the end of January nine airships attacked the country. There were seventy deaths and 113 injured. The raiders did not escape entirely unscathed. The *L19* ran low on petrol, came down too low and was fired on by anti-aircraft guns. It eventually crashed into the North Sea. An armed trawler, the *King Stephen*, came across it, with the German crew asking for help. The trawler's captain, fearing that the larger airship crew could take over his boat, left them. The airship sank and the crew drowned, giving the Germans a propaganda weapon to use against the British.

In his book of memoirs, *Sagittarius Rising*, Cecil Lewis describes how he had been interested in flying since he was a boy. Along with many others, the war gave him a chance to fly. He tried to join the RFC when he was seventeen, but then the entry age was changed to eighteen. He argued that as he had tried to join before this rule came into force it should not apply, and he was eventually accepted.

Lewis spent six weeks training at Brooklands, learning to fly on what he described as 'a museum piece'. It was a Maurice Farman Longhorn. He was then posted to Gosport, where the RFC members were billeted in an old star-shaped coastal fort. In March, Lewis was sent to France; he had just turned eighteen.

In February 1916, Leefe Robinson was sent to Hornchurch in Essex as a member of No. 39 Home Defence Squadron. There were six aircraft in the squadron, all BE2cs. There were two at each airfield – Hornchurch, Hainault Farm and North Weald. They carried a Lewis gun and a Very pistol. The pilots were flying at night and when they wanted to land they would fire the Very pistol and the ground staff would light flares to show them the runway. There was also another scheme to help the pilot see how close he was to the ground. They would let out a string with a weight on the end of it, which set off a light and buzzer when it hit the ground, showing how close they were. It was not popular with pilots and its use did not really catch on.

Lieutenant Walter Richard Gaynor RFC.

The question of how the RNAS and the RFC could work together and the problems with the supply of aircraft was raised by Major General Sir David Henderson, the General Officer of the Royal Flying Corps, in February. He stated that although there had been conferences as to the duties of the RFC and the RNAS there had never been general instructions as to the duties to be undertaken by each service during a war. Some duties were obvious, such as the RNAS service with the fleets and the RFC with the Expeditionary Force. It was in Home Defence that the real problems presented themselves, with the danger of duplication between both services.

Major General Henderson pressed home the point that there was an obvious reason for conflict between the two services. There was only a limited amount of aircraft materials to go round, especially engines. Lack of engines was seriously affecting the military air service.

The outbreak of war had led to an agreement between the Director of Air Services at the Admiralty and the Director General of Military Aeronautics.

Lieutenant Gaynor with his Fe2d aircraft, probably somewhere in Essex.

The Navy were given preference with regard to high-powered engines. This was because they were needed for seaplanes, which were heavier than land planes. This then led to the assumption that the Army would be given preference with regard to lighter engines.

Early in the war, however, the RNAS also began to acquire large numbers of land aeroplanes for the Home Defence. This meant that the Army then had serious problems obtaining enough engines for the needed expansion of the RFC. This was especially true with regard to engines from France.

One of the examples of this was the Sopwith aircraft. The company had entered into exclusive contracts with the Admiralty. This meant that it was very difficult for the RFC to get any Sopwith aircraft.

As the war continued it became evident that land aircraft also needed more powerful engines to increase their speed. Although orders had been placed for them early in the war, they were still not available in large numbers due to the lack of new designs reaching the production stage. Meanwhile, the RNAS were using many of the available powerful engines for land planes rather than seaplanes.

The Admiralty had in the previous month asked fourteen aircraft manufacturers to take part in a competition to produce high-powered land aircraft. Three of these companies had already been allotted to provide machines for the War Office for the duration of the war through an agreement with the Admiralty. Another three were already well advanced on projects similar to those the Admiralty had asked for.

Major General Henderson then went on to ask the War Council to consider what the immediate duties of the RNAS were. What were the immediate duties of the RFC? What was the order of importance of these duties? And lastly, what was the best way to distribute the available materials? The problems between the two air services were to continue throughout the war.

Before the war, the Air Committee had been established as an intermediary between the War Office and the Admiralty. It lacked any authority to impose its will and was of little use. It therefore did not meet again after the war began. The supply problems between the two air services had become serious by this point, and at the War Committee meeting in February, it was decided to establish the Joint War Air Committee to sort out these problems.

The chairman of the committee was to be Lord Derby and it would be a joint naval and army organization to co-ordinate the design and supply of aircraft materials. Unfortunately, the new committee had no more powers than the pre-war Air Committee. Lord Curzon had by this time already suggested the formation of an air ministry to solve the problems.

In March, Lord Montagu made a speech at the House of Commons about the situation in relation to the air services. He asked whether an important service such as the Air Service could afford to be administered by two government departments, the Admiralty and the War Office, who were traditionally rivals for money, men and materials. There had to be concentration of administration to secure concentration of policy. He hoped, therefore, that the Lord Derby committee would be supported as forerunner of a ministry of aviation.

An article in *Flight* magazine on 16 March stated that Lord Derby was a man who stood high in the estimation of his countrymen despite not being a member of the Cabinet. However, the article went on to report that in a recent speech by Derby in the House he was minimizing the importance of the committee. What this meant was that Lord Derby had no influence over the defence of the country against air raids.

The following edition of *Flight* magazine, on 23 March, mentioned how Lord Montagu in the House of Lords was calling for the formation of an air ministry and had asked Lord Derby what the functions of the new Joint War Air Committee would be. It seems that instead of answering the question, the prime minister invited Montagu to join the committee.

The report went on to state that the actual lack of co-operation between the two air services meant that a number of machines needed by one group were standing idle in the airfields of the other. According to the report, this situation was not known to the government or the public and would have caused a sensation if it had been public knowledge.

The *L15* was brought down in the Thames in April 1916 by, it was decided, a combination of the guns at Purfleet, Abbey Wood and Erith, as well as Alfred Brandon from Hainault Airfield, who dropped bombs on an airship on the same evening.

Of course, as the Joint War Air Committee had no powers, it was doomed to failure, and after only eight meetings Lord Derby resigned. He said that it seemed impossible to bring the two air services together unless they were amalgamated into one. Despite this being the consensus, no one was strong enough to force the issue with the Admiralty and the War Office.

There were more attempts at protecting the country from air raids and the RNAS used balloons around the coast to watch for enemy airships. This, of course, was only effective in the daytime and, as most raids were at night, they did little good. More anti-aircraft guns were deployed around the coast but there were still not enough searchlights.

The development of new flying actions continued. There was an experiment carried out at Kingsnorth on the Isle of Grain, in February. An airship took off with a BE2c slung beneath it. It was an attempt to launch an aircraft from an airship. The aircraft was manned by Squadron Commander Ireland and Wing Commander Usborne. The experiment was a disaster. At 400 feet the aircraft's nose dropped due to a lack of pressure in the airship. One of the crew fell out to his death. The aircraft was then released and because the nose had dropped, crashed straight into the river below, killing the other crewmember.

Although most air raids were carried out by airship at this stage of the war some German aircraft also attacked. In February, two German seaplanes bombed Lowestoft and Walmer. British aircraft did take off but by then the enemy had gone and the anti-aircraft guns fired on the British aircraft.

Although the aircraft were there to defend against the bombing by Zeppelins there was little they could do to stop them. Anti-aircraft fire was more effective and one airship, the *L15*, was brought down in the Thames in April 1916. There was some debate as to who actually brought the airship down. Several batteries of guns along the Thames claimed responsibility. However, a pilot from Hainault Farm Airfield, Alfred de Bath Brandon, was awarded the DSO for dropping bombs on a Zeppelin while his aircraft was riddled with machine-gun fire. This was on the same evening that the *L15* came down.

In May there was another attempt to establish co-operation between the RFC and the RNAS with the formation of the Air Board. The chairman was Lord Curzon, who was a Cabinet minister. It was hoped that having someone from such a high position in control would give the board a greater standing than the previous organizations aimed at the same objective.

The Sopwith Pups were successful in Europe in 1916 but as they became outclassed by German aircraft, they were mainly transferred to Home Defence.

There were fewer attacks in the early summer months of 1916, as the nights were not long enough for the airships to get across the sea and back again without being seen. Not that it made much difference, as there seemed to be little that could be done to stop them if they were seen unless they were hit by AA fire.

From his surviving private papers in the Imperial War Museum, we learn that C. Bartlett joined the RNAS in 1916 and went to train at the old Franco British Exhibition centre at White City. There was no flying there, however, and he went to Chingford to learn to fly. He said that the airfield was far from ideal as there were too many streams, even though they had been boarded over. Ben Travers, who became a famous playwright and novelist after the war, was also there at the time.

In August, Bartlett then went to Eastchurch, where he was trained on Lewis guns and bombs at the aerodrome at Leysdown. When he finally set out from Dover to France he had to change from the blue naval uniform to khaki.

The dramatic change in the fortunes of the Zeppelin hunters came in September 1916, when they began to use different bullets. This is often credited to the Pomeroy exploding bullet. Pomeroy was a New Zealander who was living in Australia. He had invented an exploding bullet in 1902 that had been ignored by the New Zealand Government. He presented it to the

British War Office in August 1914, but again it was ignored until September 1916, when the War Office finally showed some interest.

There was also another exploding bullet, invented in 1915 by Commander Frederick Brock of the Royal Navy. Both the bullets were used together in the Lewis guns that armed the aircraft. There was later some dispute over whose bullets were more effective against airships. It seems that the Pomeroy bullets only worked when hitting a hard surface, which against a Zeppelin wasn't assured.

In early September there were warnings from lightships in the North Sea about a large group of airships on their way to attack London. They began to bomb London on 3 September and the aircraft took off to find them. Leefe Robinson saw an airship over Woolwich and began to attack it, but lost it in the clouds. He then found another, the *SL11*, over Victoria Park in Hackney.

ZEPPELIN BROUGHT DOWN IN FLAMES
AT CUFFLEY, NEAR ENFIELD, AT 2.30 A.M., SUNDAY SEPT 3rd 1916.
(DRAWN BY AN EYE-WITNESS)

A postcard produced to commemorate the shooting down of the airship at Cuffley by Lieutenant Leefe Robinson on 3 September 1916.

He emptied all his ammunition into the airship without there seeming to be any effect. Then suddenly, it burst into flames.

The burning airship was visible all over London. A number of people had been watching Leefe Robinson attack it in his BE2c. They saw the airship coming down and there was loud cheering all over the city. The airship eventually crashed to earth at Cuffley.

Thousands of people travelled to the site of the crash to look at the wreckage and the bodies of the crew, who had all died. It was evident from the wreckage that the ship had been wooden-framed. The War Office tried to capitalize on this by claiming that it was because the Germans were short of aluminium. There was also a false explanation given to the public of how the airship was brought down. It was said that it was due to incendiary bombs dropped on the ship from above. They no doubt wished to keep the real method of the exploding bullets secret.

The *SL11* was the first Zeppelin to be brought down over the mainland. The *Essex Weekly News* reported that the residents of Romford, and no doubt Dagenham and Barking, had a beautiful view of the falling Zeppelin.

There seems to have been very little compassion for the crew. During the funeral eggs were thrown at their coffins by the public. The RFC members showed more respect than the public. It was members of the RFC who carried

The wreckage of the downed airship at Cuffley. Inset, Lieutenant Leefe Robinson, who shot it down.

the coffins of the German crew of the airship. They were buried at Potter's Bar. The bodies of the crew were carried on a lorry and the commander's body in a separate car. One of the officers who carried the commander's coffin was Lieutenant A. de B. Brandon MC.

There was a lot of compassion for Lieutenant Leefe Robinson. He was sent gifts of money totalling over £4,000. He was also awarded the Victoria Cross by the king at Windsor Castle. Leefe Robinson became an overnight celebrity, with his photograph displayed in newspapers, magazines and on postcards.

Bomb damage to the Sphinx on Thames Embankment. The marks from the bomb can still be seen on the statue.

It seems strange that Leefe Robinson should have gained so much fame over others who had done the same as him in bringing down airships. Perhaps it was because his had been witnessed by so many members of the public. It was good for morale.

Two weeks later, Leefe Robinson crashed his aircraft on take-off, the one he had used on the night he shot down the airship. The plane burst into flames and was destroyed. The government panicked at the thought of losing their new hero who could do so much for morale. Luckily, Leefe Robinson survived the crash and was then sent on a series of public appearances instead of being allowed to fly.

Now that an airship had been shot down it seemed as if their previous invincibility had vanished. On the night of 23/24 September, a Zeppelin bombed the airfield at Hornchurch. Then Fred Sowery, based at the airfield, shot down the *L32* at Billericay. On the same evening, the *L33* was hit by anti-aircraft fire and was then attacked and further damaged by Alfred de Bath Brandon from Hainault. After going out to sea the airship turned back and landed near Colchester.

The crew survived and burnt their airship before surrendering to a local constable. That was two airships brought down on the same night and one of them was the second victory credited to a pilot from Hornchurch. The story of the Hornchurch pilots was still not over. On 1 October, Lieutenant Tempest, also from Hornchurch, shot down another airship, the *L31*, over Potter's Bar. There were two more Zeppelins destroyed in November – one

The wreckage of the Zeppelin brought down by Lieutenant Sowery on 24 September 1916, at Billericay in Essex.

The gondolas and propellers of the Zeppelin shot down by Lieutenant Sowery. The wreckage narrowly missed landing on the town of Billericay.

near Hartlepool and the other near Lowestoft. The seemingly invincible Zeppelin menace may have been damaged but worse was yet to come, and the airship threat was still not finished.

There were still constant differences of opinion over the best way to produce the aircraft needed to fight the war. A memorandum had been circulated to the War Committee in September from a Mr Montagu stating that the Ministry of Munitions had achieved a great output of standard equipment in a short time and this could also be done by them in the case of aircraft.

The plan put forward was that the War Office should retain control of design and experiment of aircraft while the Royal Aircraft Factory should be handed over to the Ministry of Munitions. The only view agreed on by both sides was that it was wrong to continue to allow the Admiralty and the War Office to persist in competing to acquire aircraft.

The Air Board contested Mr Montagu's view that this was what the flying services required. The Air Board's view was based on the demands of

General Trenchard (the commander of the RFC until 1917, and then Chief of Air Staff) and Field Marshal Haig (the commander of the BEF from 1915 until the end of the war), who wanted not quantity of aircraft but improved performance – vital to the struggle for aerial supremacy. General Trenchard was concerned about two new German aircraft that were better in certain respects than anything that the British had.

The view from the Air Board was that they were developing fresh engines and aircraft that would be superior to the German machines, but the question was, would they be developed in time? The development of the Fokker had put the British at a disadvantage for some time and the Air Board believed that this kind of struggle would be repeated throughout the war.

To be successful the designers and manufacturers had to work closely with the Flying Corps, who were using the machines. The manufacturers also needed flexibility to allow for variation and modification, which did not sit well alongside efforts to produce great numbers of aircraft in the shortest possible time. In October, the Air Board also published a report that was critical of the arrangements in the British air services. This was nothing new as this kind of criticism had been made from the beginning of the war. The report stated that the Army were ready to take part in meetings whereas the Navy were frequently absent and would often not provide the information they were asked for.

There seemed to be an endless succession of reports from different departments arguing their cases for control of aircraft production. Another memorandum appeared in November from the Minister of Munitions, once again arguing its case in reply to the report from the Air Board.

Now there was not only conflict between the Admiralty and the Army in relation to aviation but also between the Air Board and the Ministry of Munitions. The organization of flying during the war was crying out for one body to take control but no one in the government appeared to be willing to take such a step or give anyone the power to force the conflicting sides into agreement.

The Minister of Munitions argued, along with others, that the continued competition for aircraft between the two air services was not a sensible way to proceed. Then it would be down to the War Committee to decide who should control a single supply service. He maintained that the Ministry of Munitions should be in control, as they were already responsible for supplying other munitions of war. One of the reasons they had been created was to solve the problem of supplies running short of demand.

The three Zeppelin slayers of Suttons Farm, Hornchurch. From left: Robinson, Tempest and Sowery.

The Air Board, however, argued that the constant change in design of aircraft needed discussion between the men using the machines and the manufacturers producing them. They did not go on to elaborate why the Ministry of Munitions could not do this in a similar way to the Air Board.

It seems as if the same arguments were going back and forth between different agencies, all trying to gain control of the production of aircraft. One must wonder how much of this was due to the egos of the men wanting to be in control and how much was actually due to the ambition to solve the problem of supply and demand of aircraft for the war effort.

Despite the disputes in government the public were still very interested in flying. The Lord Mayor's Show in London in November had an understandably military bias. Included in the procession was a German field

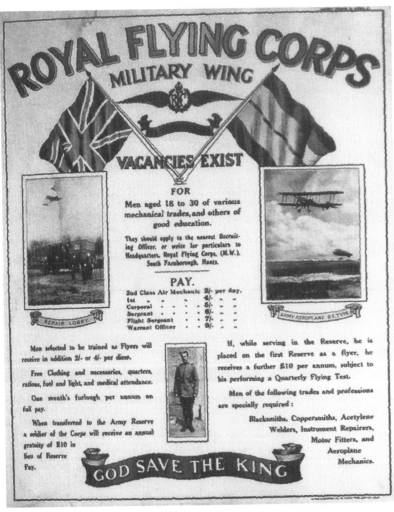

A recruiting poster for the RFC. It wasn't only pilots that were wanted, but men of all trades.

gun captured in France and a German aircraft minus its wings but still with the black crosses painted on its sides.

The celebrity status achieved by Leefe Robinson was beginning to be a mixed blessing. For their success, on 14 October both he and Sowery were to be presented with silver cups at Grey Towers camp, a local army camp in Hornchurch. Then Tempest shot down his airship and they had to have another cup made. By then, Leefe Robinson was fed up with not being able to fly. He asked for a transfer back to France and was told that he may have to go to a posting in the north of England.

Fatalities did not only occur in Europe, as the gravestone of Flight Lieutenant Hardstaff in Eastchurch churchyard shows. Hardstaff had been on the Admiralty aero testing staff. While testing a new engine, the tailplane failed, leading to his death.

It was in the north, on 27 October, that the next Zeppelin met its fate. Ten airships attacked and the *L34* was shot down by Second Lieutenant Pyott RFC off West Hartlepool.

By this time the British had finally produced a bomber of their own. The Handley Page 0/100 was flown by the RNAS. It was used for bombing in Europe. The aircraft was then developed into the 1/400, which was much more widely used.

There had also been a bomber built by de Havilland/Airco in 1916. The DH3 was a two-engined pusher but it never went into production. De Havilland did, however, build other bombers that went into use later.

There was now a testing squadron based at Upavon in Wiltshire, where they tested all the aircraft produced. There was still not a very good knowledge of the design of aircraft and every new one was an experiment. Many were still made by private companies.

Leefe Robinson wasn't the only flying celebrity in the country. In November 1916, Albert Ball DSO, who at the age of twenty had shot down more than thirty German aircraft, was awarded the freedom of Nottingham. Ball was the son of a previous mayor of the city. He was treated to lunch by the current mayor, Councillor Small. Ball presented photographs of himself to the mayor and the sheriff in frames made from the tips of propellers from the enemy aircraft he had shot down.

There had by this time been some more attacks by aircraft; one bombed London in broad daylight in November 1916. The year 1916 saw some important developments in the war in the air. Although the Air Committee had been formed early in the year it had given up after little more than a month. There were still apparent problems between the RFC and RNAS as the RFC had mainly Royal Air Force Factory designed machines while the RNAS had more privately designed aircraft, which were often superior.

There were a number of developments that took place in 1916 that were to improve the lot of the British pilots, including the redesign of both Vickers and Lewis machine guns to make them more suitable for use in the air. The following year was also to see a better organization of the resources for the flying service.

Nineteen-seventeen

In January, Lord Curzon was replaced by Lord Cowdray as the chairman of the Air Board. The holder of the newly created post of Fifth Sea Lord and

Director of Naval Aviation, Godfrey Paine, now sat on the board. High-level representation from the Navy did help to improve matters in relation to the level of co-operation between the air services but did not entirely solve the problems.

Paine had a great deal of experience of flying and was himself a qualified pilot. He had been the first commandant of the Flying School at Upavon in 1912. He was then the commodore at the new Central Depot and Training Establishment at Cranwell from 1915.

Despite the involvement of a high-ranking naval officer on the Air Board, the problems were not completely solved, which led to greater government discussions, especially between the prime minister and General Smuts. It seemed that there were constant discussions about the problems with the air services but very little action.

At the beginning of 1917, the RNAS had more than 1,000 aircraft and 400 seaplanes. These included forty-three different types of aircraft, and of these, fifteen were the same kind of machines that the RFC had. The RNAS used thirty-nine different types of engines and the RFC thirty. There were fifty-seven different types of engines across the two services. This often led to problems in obtaining spare parts as there were so many variations.

The use of aircraft in war was of great interest to the public and this was exploited by the Countess of Drogheda. She arranged an aircraft exhibition

Felixstowe was the site of an RNAS base during the war. This photograph shows an early seaplane on the beach.

A seaplane flying over Felixstowe, where the RNAS base was. Although in Felixstowe, it was often called Harwich.

at the Grosvenor Gallery in Bond Street, London, to show the progress in aircraft design during its relatively short history. This included artefacts from Zeppelins destroyed by the RFC and the RNAS, who lent them to the exhibition. There were also official photographs relating to aviation from the Admiralty and the War Office.

The exhibition was not arranged with personal gain in mind as the proceeds from the entrance fees were to be divided between the flying services and the Irish Hospital Supply Depots. These were operating under the direction of the Red Cross Society.

The government decided in early 1917 that it would release all men between eighteen and twenty-two years of age from munitions work for call-up to the Army. This caused some problems in the production of munitions, including aircraft assembly. The call-up included skilled men who had been involved in the production of aeroplanes and aeronautical woodwork.

The effect on some companies such as Vickers would, it was argued, be enormous. V. Calliard, the director of Vickers, wrote to the Ministry of Munitions claiming that at their Barrow works, production would fall between thirty and sixty-five per cent. At Sheffield, the whole works would be paralysed. It would cripple production at Erith, paralyse Crayford, cripple Beyer Peacock and cause a serious reduction at Electric & Ordnance Co. Ltd. The director then went on to withdraw all promises of delivery dates to the ministry due to the government's actions.

The Air Board did try to alleviate some of the difficulties caused by the new round of military call-ups. The Controller of Aeronautical Supplies stated that it would be impossible to ask for exemption from service for all men engaged on aeronautical production as this would cover too much ground. However, a list of special trades had been drawn up and this was to be submitted to the committee in the hope of gaining exemption for the most important workers.

The Air Board was also trying to define its duties in relation to the Admiralty, the War Office and the Ministry of Munitions, and in February sent a letter and memo to the War Cabinet. This was in answer to a Cabinet meeting in December in which the duties of the Air Board were outlined. The Cabinet had decided that the details of the duties of all four organizations should be worked out by discussions between them – which is what had been going on since the war had begun. The government was worried that they were making decisions that seemed to be based on little knowledge of aircraft. It seems unbelievable that after more than two years at war there were problems in relation to the air service that were still only being discussed and not dealt with.

The Cabinet had decided that the design as well as the production of aircraft should be given to the Ministry of Munitions. The ministry as a manufacturing or supply department did not consider itself adapted to deal with the highly specialized duty of selecting and approving the design of aircraft. They argued that the science of aeronautics was in such a state of rapid and constant growth that it should be in the hands of a body on which the air services were represented. It was therefore agreed that this should be the Air Board.

It was also agreed that the Cabinet decision that aircraft should be designed by the Ministry of Munitions and seaplanes by the Admiralty should not be insisted upon. The two types of aircraft were manufactured by the same companies and built out of the same raw materials. Design presented similar problems. They should therefore both be designed by the same source.

The memo went on to suggest that the Air Board should include representatives from the Admiralty, the War Office and the Ministry of Munitions. This would mean that the Admiralty and War Office would discuss their aerial policies with the Air Board. The board would then decide

A Short seaplane on the river Blackwater, in Essex. (Courtesy of James Payne, Through Their Eyes)

to what extent these policies were feasible in relation to the needs of each department.

There would be a technical committee under the direction of the board to design aircraft and engines. The naval and military experimental air stations, while staying under the administrative control of the Admiralty and the Army, would be under the control of the technical committee.

The Royal Aircraft Factory would be placed under the control of the Ministry of Munitions. They would, however, permit the facilities of the factory to be utilized by the Technical Committee for experiments. The Ministry of Munitions would then be responsible for producing the aircraft.

In February 1917, Leefe Robinson finally got his wish to return to active duty. He was posted to Rendcomb, in Gloucestershire, and in March flew with seventeen others in Bristol Fighters to Bertangles, in France.

The attempts to reduce the number of different types of engines and aircraft in use had begun to be effective by March. The total number of engine types in use had been reduced to thirty-three. The aircraft models were reduced to thirty-nine and the seaplanes to sixteen. Not only did this help make the service more reliable for the supply of parts, but it also meant that the most reliable machines were becoming the more common.

A report from the Air Board in March stated that it had been decided to set up a special expert committee to investigate the causes of accidents occurring

There were numerous ideas put forward by towns to raise money for the war effort. Brentwood had an aeroplane week to try and raise enough money to buy an aircraft.

BRENTWOOD
Aeroplane Week
begins next
MONDAY

IF, during the week beginning next Monday, the subscriptions from Brentwood for National War Bonds and War Savings Certificates reach the total of £35,000, the authorities will give to an Aeroplane the name of our town.

Think of our civic pride if we read in an official despatch that

the Aeroplane
"BRENTWOOD"

has carried the war into German territory and harried the lines of communication of the foe—perhaps that it has saved Brentwood men from the deadly attack of the Hun, enabling them to return unharmed to their wives and children.

Do your duty during
Brentwood Aeroplane Week

Have your money ready for Monday—ready to buy National War Bonds and War Savings Certificates — ready to help in making Brentwood Aeroplane Week a triumphant, a record success.

Get your Pass Book. See how much money you have in the Bank. Draw the cheque and have it ready to give Brentwood's effort a flying start on Monday morning.

in the experimental stages of aircraft. They were considering setting up a central design establishment under the board for the trial of new engines put forward by manufacturers. The problem with this was that it would be another way of inspiring distrust by manufacturers, which was the case when the Royal Aircraft Factory did this. It would, therefore, be better if manufacturers set up their own testing benches. There seemed to be constant backtracking on ideas to improve the service if any new plans upset anyone.

May 1917 was to be an eventful month in the war in the air. On the 14th, a Curtis flying boat with a crew of three flown by Flight Commander Leckie RNAS shot down the *L22* near Terschelling. All the crew died. There was also an attack on shipping off the east coast by German aircraft using torpedoes. The third airship raid of the year also took place.

Postcards showing the downfall of German airships were very popular with the public.

It was also to be the month when the full force of Germany's new weapon came into play and began to bomb the capital. The Gotha was a twin-engined aircraft with a 77-foot wingspan. It had a crew of three, was armed with two machine guns and carried between 600lbs and 1,100lbs of bombs. The first Gotha attack on the capital failed due to the weather.

General Trenchard's pamphlet published in 1916 had described aircraft as offensive rather than defensive weapons. This then meant that the German bombers had the upper hand. He stated that defensive duties were based more on promoting morale than on restricting damage. This seemed to be born out when, on 30 May, air mechanics at Hythe were stoned by members of the public because of the air raids. This was despite the fact that the aircraft based there were for training purposes rather than for the Home Defence.

Someone who was impressed with the training going on for airmen at home was the king. He visited Hendon Aerodrome at the end of May. A photograph of him appeared in *The Illustrated War News* congratulating Captain B.C. Hucks, who had looped the loop twice in one minute in front of His Majesty.

Just as the Zeppelins had at first been immune to attack from Home Defence fighters, so were the Gothas. They flew so high that it took the fighters too long to get high enough to attack so that the enemy had already flown off by the time they did. Another problem was that once the Zeppelin danger had been disposed of the Home Defence forces had been slashed by half.

The danger of attack by aircraft became evident on 25 May, when a daylight raid on Folkestone by sixteen German aircraft took place. They flew at a very great height and dropped bombs in a number of parts of the town, including a busy shopping street. Twenty-seven women and twenty-

Behold the end of a raiding " Gotha,"
A prey to Kentish fire.
Our boys at the guns have finished the Huns
And lit their funeral pyre.

A Gotha falling, with a patriotic poem on the postcard.

three children were killed in the attack and many others were injured. The total was seventy-four deaths and 174 injuries. The raiders were pursued by RFC aircraft and then attacked by RNAS aircraft from Dunkirk. Three of the enemy aircraft were shot down.

Some squadrons were called back from France to meet the threat of the new bombers. One of these was 56 Squadron, who were based at Bekesbourne, near Canterbury. No further raids took place during the next two weeks and the squadron was sent back to France.

As soon as enemy aircraft were spotted approaching the coast, warnings would be given to the police, fire service and some factories in London. The problem then was that the aircraft might bomb some other part of the country and there would be no raid on London. This had happened on a number of occasions when warnings were given and no attack then took place, suspending normal life in London for no reason.

This led to the argument that warnings could actually increase the dangers to the public, such as people rushing into the street to watch attacks, the workforce of large factories leaving their work premises, and mothers rushing to schools to get their children. Of course, repeated warnings resulting in no raids would then lead to the public ignoring them altogether.

A deputation of London mayors suggested that the initial warning when aircraft crossed the coast should only be given to the police and fire services. A public warning would then only be given if it was clear that an attack was aimed at London.

The argument against this was that because the aircraft flew so high they were not always seen when crossing the coast, or if they were, they may not be seen again until they were already over London. Also, if they crossed the coast at Southend it would be necessary to warn London straight away because they would get there so quickly, but again, they may not be headed for London.

The newly arrived flying boats of the RNAS were proving to be very useful. One had already shot down an airship in May, and on 14 June, another Curtiss from Felixstowe shot down the *L43*. The aircraft had a crew of four and was flown by Lieutenant Hobbs.

A few days later, airships bombed Ramsgate and Martlesham. It was the *L48* that bombed Martlesham and it was then shot down. It had been on its maiden flight. The pilot who shot it down was Second Lieutenant L. Watkins, a Canadian RFC pilot from Goldhanger Airfield. He was aided by

Air raid warnings during the First World War were not very high profile, as can be seen from this photograph.

Captain R. Saundby from Orford Ness. The airship landed near Theberton in Suffolk, and some of the crew survived.

There were often still problems for the pilots in finding the airships once they had taken off. There was now a new form of attack. Although the land-based pilots would often take off during a raid, the seaplanes and flying boats of the RNAS would try and catch the airships the following morning as they returned home.

There was a meeting on 31 May to discuss the defence of the United Kingdom from attack by aircraft. Lieutenant General Sir David Henderson said that the policy that had been laid down by the War Committee in February 1915 was that the Navy were to deal with any aircraft attempting to reach Britain while the Army dealt with any that did. By this time the system had changed so that the RNAS gave information of impending raids and intercepted the enemy on their return.

The meeting considered that with about four hours' flying time the enemy aircraft could reach points on the coast between Southwold and Rottingdean, and inland with a line from Bury St Edmunds to Brentford, and then down to Rottingdean. It was not considered likely that raids would take place north of Southwold.

Warnings of raids were sent from seaplanes with radios, which could communicate with Westgate and Felixstowe, from where messages were sent direct to the Admiralty air exchange. Messages were also sent from lightships. It was suggested that trained observers be placed on lightships.

The Admiralty undertook to instruct the RFC at Dunkirk to watch the enemy aerodromes at Ghistelle, near Ostende, and St Denis West, near Loos, for any unusual movement of enemy aircraft. They also considered whether it was feasible for extended patrols to collect more information. During the raid of 25 May it took thirteen minutes for the message to be relayed from the *Tongue* lightship to the Home Forces; the message had to go through four transmitting stations. There were attempts to find out where the delay occurred and what could be done to ensure faster transmission of warnings.

Once the message reached the Home Forces it was passed to the commanding Home Defence group and the squadrons very quickly. But information of where the raiders were once they crossed the coast was defective. Ways to improve this defect were to be examined.

The RNAS patrolled from Sheerness to Maplin Sands, Westgate to Barrow Lightship, and Felixstowe to Barrow lightship, North Foreland to Walmer, Felixstowe to North Hinder and Lowestoft to Terschelling. The patrols were undertaken by seaplanes.

It was stated that it would be wasteful and uneconomical to send fighting machines over the sea to intercept the enemy. The only fighting machines that the RNAS had were at Manstone, Walmer and Dover, where a varying number of aircraft were always available. This was normally about six at each base.

The RFC had aircraft ready to deal with Zeppelins but during the recent aircraft raid there were only twenty-two aircraft available to the Home Forces for daytime raids. To increase this, training brigades were being moved into the areas in danger. Orford Ness and Martlesham Heath experimental stations were being organized to protect north Essex and the river Blackwater.

Once the plans were in place there would be forty machines to patrol round London, seventeen from Goldhanger to Detling, eight from Chiddingstone to Marden and Hastings to Romney, and six from Dover to Broadsalts. There would also be ten machines between Throwley and Bekesbourne. This gave a total of fifty-nine machines. Unfortunately, they were training machines and only fifty per cent could be relied upon at any one time.

A BE2e at Stow Maries, in Essex. The men are swinging the propeller to start the engine
(Courtesy of James Payne, Through Their Eyes)

There was discussion between the Air Board, the War Cabinet and the
Ministry of Munitions in June on the production of aircraft over the next
twelve months. The Air Board said that it hoped to increase the output of
engines so that by January 1918 it would be producing 2,200 a month.

One of the problems they had was that at that time the output of aircraft
still exceeded the number of machine guns available to arm them. The
Master General of Ordnance did, however, have the matter in hand.

If a large output of aircraft was to be achieved, orders had to be placed a long
time ahead for the types of aircraft that were likely to meet the requirements
of the flying services without too many modifications. This was already the
case with training machines, which were practically standardized. This
was also the case with reconnaissance machines. The board was therefore
considering large orders of these types of machines.

There had obviously been great improvement in the number of machines
produced. The report from the Air Board gave the figures for the month of
May 1916 as 270 engines and 304 aircraft produced. For May 1917 it was
853 engines and 1,202 aircraft.

It was to be June before the new German bombers finally carried out a
successful attack on London during the day. One of the worst incidents of
the raid was when a school in Poplar was hit and at least sixteen children
died. After this the German raids came during the night.

Regular raids began again with a large raid on London in mid-June. The bombed areas were visited by the king shortly after the raids took place. His Majesty, accompanied by Lord Cromer and Major Reginald Seymour, visited the hospitals where the injured had been taken.

A few days later, fifteen funerals of the children killed at school during the earlier raid took place in Poplar. They were buried in the East London Cemetery, a venue not unused to seeing the result of East End disasters. A sixteenth coffin contained body parts of children unidentified. The funeral procession was accompanied by soldiers who marched alongside the coffins.

The burials were marked by more than 500 wreaths sent from individuals and organizations from all across the country, many of whom also sent representatives to the funerals. The horror of the results of the raid on innocent children had been deeply felt throughout the country. The bishop of London said that this was the most touching sight he had seen in his twenty-eight years of working in the capital. He also called for military action against the places where the raiders came from.

There was a meeting held in June between Sir George Cave and Lieutenant Colonel Laud of the General Staff Home Forces. It was to decide if warnings would be given in London in the event of air raids. The system that had been in operation was obviously not working.

In June, there was an interesting request from the Dominion Government of New Zealand to the War Office. They wanted to know if there would be any objection to candidates of Maori blood from Canterbury Aviation School applying for admission to the RFC. The War Office replied that they had no objection.

Another raid on London took place on 7 July, but this time the raiders did not have it all their own way. Second Lieutenant John Young flew straight into the middle of twenty-two enemy aircraft and opened fire on them. Each of the German aircraft had four guns and so he was terribly outnumbered and was shot down. Young was only nineteen and had been a member of the Artist Rifles before joining the RFC.

There was a meeting of the War Cabinet on 11 July, when it was decided that the prime minster and General Smuts would meet with the Admiralty and the commander-in-chief Home Forces to discuss the defence against air raids and the organization of aerial operations. It says a lot as to how the organization was formed in that the RNAS, although an important part of the Home Defence system, did not come under the command of the Home Defence chief.

The War Cabinet stated that London was the nerve centre of the Empire and that its defence demanded exceptional measures. They decided that it was probable that air raids would increase to such an extent that the capital may become part of the battlefront. Therefore, special precautions for defence had to be taken for London.

The arrangements for home defence, including London, had been undergoing continual transformation, which had, at times, limited its efficiency. The defences had been set up to deal with night attacks by Zeppelins. Anti-aircraft guns in pairs or groups and aeroplanes of no great power were based at several aerodromes. This had been seen as a suitable defence against airships.

The defence against Zeppelins was found to be entirely unsuitable against attacks by large numbers of aircraft. The problem was that there was still a threat of more raids by airships as well as aeroplanes. What was needed were additions to the present system of defence while leaving Zeppelin defences in place. To meet the threat of daytime raids by large formations of aircraft larger batteries of anti-aircraft guns were needed and flights or squadrons of fighter planes to attack the enemy.

The size of German Gotha bombers must have been frightening for the public. The size of the aircraft can be gauged by the man sitting on top of the wings.

The raid of 7 July was used as an example. The enemy had attacked in formation and maintained this throughout the raid. They should have been repelled by heavy barrages from anti-aircraft guns or by a formation of defensive aircraft. What aircraft there were came in to attack in ones and twos from various bases. They did not come in formation as they had no overall command and had not been trained to fight in formation. So, despite having more aircraft than the raiders, the effect on the enemy was negligible.

Not only were the pilots lacking in the skills needed to fight large formations of bombers but some pilots were not accustomed to their new machines. A number of aircraft were not used due to a lack of spare parts and many of the shells fired by the guns had faulty fuses.

The problems were expressed in a letter from Field Marshal French, Commander-in-Chief of the Home Forces, when he wrote to the Imperial General Staff on 6 July. He was complaining that two squadrons of aircraft recently placed under his command had been withdrawn. This meant that, apart from slower machines, which had neither the climbing power nor speed to make them effective against German bombers, all he had were twelve Sopwith Scouts, three SE5s and six DH4s. There were also two aircraft at Lympne, which were too far away to be used in the defence of London.

Despite a promise of another twelve Sopwith Scouts from 15 July, the forces at his disposal were not sufficient for effective action against raids carried out in force. Such raids were to be expected and if London was

An SE5, an aircraft that was an important part of the defence against German attacks.

attacked again, the results in his opinion could have been disastrous. The fact that after three years of war only twenty-one aircraft were available to protect the capital is hard to understand.

French's letter was answered on 10 July by the War Office. It stated that the allotment of the RFC for home defence had been discussed by the War Cabinet and that one fighting squadron from France had been placed at his disposal. The squadron would not be withdrawn before this had been discussed by the War Cabinet again.

As French had asked for sixty-six machines, the letter stated that with the new squadron he would still be thirty-three aircraft short. It was hoped that twenty-four of these would be available to him by the end of the month.

The Cabinet went on to state that four separate agencies contributed to the defence of London against air raids. These were the RNAS, the Observation Corps, various units of the RFC allocated to the Home Defence and anti-aircraft guns. It seems that the principal function of the RNAS was to deal with enemy aircraft on their return across the Channel rather than stopping them from getting to their objective.

The Observation Corps were obviously not that highly regarded at the time. A comment from the Cabinet stated that 'they consisted of a number of observers round London, mostly infantry soldiers, often elderly and not especially qualified for the duties they have to perform.' It sounded as though they were allocated to this duty as they were not much use for any other task.

There was an interesting comment after this was stated. The last three agencies mentioned were operating separately under the orders of the Home Defence Headquarters, which was the only connection between them. This system involved too great a dispersal of command when dealing with air raids on London. They then called for greater control over these three agencies by the officer in command of the Home Defence.

The Cabinet comments on the RNAS were very different and once again showed the division between the air services that, it seems, were accepted by the government. The RNAS were not under the command of the Home Defence but worked under the direction of the senior naval officer in the naval districts, in co-operation, as far as possible with the Home Defence. There seemed to have been a general agreement with those consulted by the Cabinet that this division of command should not be disturbed. Once again, it appears that there was no desire to upset anyone at the Admiralty, despite saying that lack of overall command in the agencies involved in home defence was hindering efforts. According to a later statement in the Cabinet papers: 'The unity of command is essential to any warlike operation, whether of an offensive or defensive character.' It seems that the government could say one thing while closing its eyes to the fact that the opposite was occurring.

There was to be no removal of the anti-aircraft guns in place against Zeppelins. Rather it was hoped to find more guns capable of putting up a barrage against formations of enemy planes. Despite the shortage of guns, London was a special case.

The more pressing problem was the provision of a number of air units trained to fight in formation and their proper disposition to defend London. The only unit formed for this purpose was at the Western Front, and it was then to return to England. I believe it was 46 Squadron. There were three other units being formed at the time. They did not have enough aircraft nor did the pilots have sufficient training. There was another squadron with enough aircraft ready to be posted to London but the pilots still needed training. Another unit would be ready for posting within the next four weeks.

The Cabinet members were also not sure if the aircraft currently available were suitable for action against the Gothas. They were prepared to leave this question in the hands of the Air Board, the Admiralty, the War Office and the Ministry of Munitions.

There was also a worry that the enemy may send small raiding parties to draw the defensive aircraft into the air. Then the main raiding party would arrive. By this time the defending aircraft would have had to have landed to refuel – a process that would take at least forty-five minutes. This would leave the way open for unmolested attacks by the enemy. It was therefore recommended that not all the defensive units should be sent up at the first sign of a raid.

The numbers of aircraft available for the defence of London needed to be large enough to deal with feints and then to meet the real attack. This would entail the formation and retention of a reserve. If the suggested points were fulfilled then the security of London would be achieved.

Harwich and Felixstowe was the scene of an air raid on the morning of 22 July. The director of military intelligence reported to the War Cabinet that seven soldiers and one male civilian had died. Twenty soldiers and three male civilians had been wounded. One of the German raiders had been brought down over the sea.

Squadron Commander A.F. Betterton of the RNAS was shot down by a German Gotha in August 1917 while flying a Sopwith Camel, but survived. Unfortunately, he was then killed the following month while flying. His grave is in Eastchurch churchyard, in Kent.

The deputy chief of naval staff said that no extensive damage had been done to the area. There had been twenty-five RNAS aircraft that had taken off during the raid. Major General Shaw explained to the Cabinet that there had been no air fighting involving the RFC on the 22nd as the enemy aircraft had merely touched the coast before their formation was broken by anti-aircraft fire. They therefore did not penetrate inland.

There had by this time been a move back towards aircraft being carried by ships. As early as 1912, Lieutenant Sampson had managed to take off in a Short S.38 T2 from ramps on HMS *Africa* at Sheerness. Some of the Harwich Destroyer Force had ramps fitted early in the war but these were taken off in 1915.

There had been a naval conference held in August 1917, which recognized the importance of air power at sea and that it was needed to combat hostile recognizance. To do this ships needed aircraft that could take off from ramps. Up until now the use of aircraft at sea was mainly restricted to

Before aircraft carriers, aircraft would be carried on lighters pulled behind destroyers. The ship would then go full speed into the wind so the aircraft, like the Sopwith Camel on this postcard, could take off.

lighters carrying seaplanes that were hoisted into the water, from where they could take off.

There was an example of what could be achieved from ship-launched aircraft when on 18 August Flight Lieutenant Smart took off from HMS *Yarmouth* in a Sopwith Pup and shot down the airship *L23*. One of the problems with aircraft flying from ships was that they then had to find the ship again afterwards. Smart eventually put down in the sea and the aircraft was salvaged by HMS *Canterbury*.

The use of aircraft by the Navy was also discussed by the War Cabinet in a meeting on 24 August. They were discussing a report from the prime minister and General Smuts on air organization and home defence.

The position of the government was clearly laid out as to the formation of an air ministry. It was admitted that air organization had been the subject of acute controversy. It had seemed to make sense in the early days of aviation to have two separate services to meet the needs of the Navy and the Army. An early war committee had been formed to ensure peace and co-operation between the two groups. On the outbreak of war the committee ceased to exist as its members went off to fight.

The committee had then been replaced by the Joint War Air Committee. This did not last as it had no actual power. This was followed by the Air Board, which was also severely limited as it was really a conference of members of the Admiralty, Army and Ministry of Munitions. The real directors of war policy in relation to flying had been the Army and the Navy, and they were not always in accord.

The government now stated, however, that the time was rapidly approaching when the subordination of the Air Board and the Air Service could no longer be justified. The air service was not just a weapon but an independent arm of the forces. Therefore there was no reason why the Air Board should not be raised to the status of an independent ministry in control of its own war service.

The suggestion then was that an air ministry should be instituted as soon as possible with a minister and a consultative board on the lines of the Admiralty Board. The ministry would control and administer all matters in connection with aerial warfare. Under the ministry an air staff would be created on the lines of the Imperial General Staff. The government had finally realized what was needed but still nothing happened straight away.

The Board of the Admiralty was of the opinion that there was a great difference between the services that the RNAS provided to the fleet and the service that the RFC provided to the Army. They argued that the Army needed good spotting and aerial reconnaissance but that a serious catastrophe would be unlikely to occur if the air service was not good. On the other hand, because of the rapidity of movement at sea, faulty aerial reconnaissance might have the gravest consequences. The use of aircraft for reconnaissance took the place of light cruisers. It was therefore essential that knowledge of naval warfare should be available to airmen in the RNAS.

This was especially true if aircraft were to be carried on-board ships. The training of the pilots and observers of the RNAS for operations with the fleet was a far more difficult process than the training of army pilots and could take twice as long. They had to recognize all types of ships. They therefore were of the opinion that the proposed air ministry should continue in the same way towards the RNAS as the Air Board did.

It seems that the Admiralty were again arguing for the retention of their independence in relation to the RNAS. The Admiralty did, however, recognize that there were reasons for a development of air policy and they accepted the views of those who had investigated it. They agreed with a future for an air offensive separate from the Navy and the Army, but it did

As the war progressed, the supply of aircraft and parts improved, as shown from this London aircraft store.

not appear practical that such operations should take place over the sea without being under naval command.

The Admiralty then suggested that the proposed air ministry should adopt its proposed functions for the Army while leaving the RNAS as it was for the moment – at least for the duration of the war. The supply of aircraft and spare parts could also be the ministry's job but training of the RNAS should stay in the hands of the Admiralty.

They did concede that the duties of the RNAS that were not totally connected with the Navy could be passed over to the Air Ministry. If this was not acceptable then they suggested that the pilots and machines for naval work could be provided by the Air Ministry but the Admiralty should have the power to approve the machines and men allocated to them. It was also important that the units given to the Admiralty should be under the control of the Admiralty. The Admiralty believed that if these conditions were not agreed to then there would be a serious danger to the fleet.

It seemed that the Admiralty were in favour of an air ministry with power over the RFC but with the same relationship to the RNAS as the Air Board already had.

Lord Curzon, president of the Air Board, argued that if the Admiralty's suggestion was accepted then the Air Ministry would have the same lack of powers as the Air Board had and there would have been no advance made. He was convinced that an air ministry with full independent powers, subject to the War Cabinet, was what was needed. If this was accepted then the amalgamation of the two air services under the new ministry could be the subject of a fresh committee, which would discuss the safeguards requested by the Admiralty and provide such safeguards as agreed by the committee.

Lord Curzon went on to argue that there was a tendency to exaggerate the differences between the air services. He said that after the war there must be a unified service under a minister to control it. Separate training of personnel could not be contemplated, although there could be different classes of training.

He believed that there was a natural rivalry between the two air services, which was prejudicial to efficiency and the proper supply and distribution of materials. It was not to be expected that there could be complete co-operation between the two services unless they were amalgamated.

The Minister of Munitions favoured the formation of an air ministry but saw many problems in the process that would not be easily solved. He believed that there were natural bonds linking the two services. There should, therefore, be no great difficulties in combining them into one service as long as there was recognition of the special needs of the Navy.

Support for the Admiralty position also came from Winston Churchill, which was no surprise considering his naval connections and his experience of flying. He agreed with the technical differences involved in the training between naval and army personnel and that the Navy airmen needed longer periods of training.

Churchill went on to explain how the Americans believed that victory would be achieved by the side that obtained mastery of the air. There had therefore been a great expansion in the output of aircraft and a diversion of skilled workers to that objective. He believed that this should be subject to the guidance of a special air war staff.

The Chief of the Imperial General Staff said that the prime minister's report had been considered by the Army and that they accepted in principal the idea of a separate air service. It should be made clear, however, that the War Office should be responsible for laying down the requirements of the Army in relation to aircraft.

It seems that, despite both the Army and the Navy accepting to some extent the idea of a unified air service, there were reservations. No doubt these were partly based on the fact that so far during the war the organizations set up to deal with the air services had been far from ideal, with constant arguments as to which organization should provide which services.

The supply of propellers was also improved as the war continued. They were made by skilled carpenters.

August also saw a raid on the Margate and Dover areas, but this wasn't as successful for the raiders because three Gothas were shot down. There were ten German aircraft in the attacking force and two were shot down by anti-aircraft fire and RFC aircraft. The other was brought down by the RNAS.

The third victim came down in the sea off the North Foreland, on the east coast of Kent between Margate and Ramsgate, and only one of the crew was found alive. The wreckage of the aircraft was later salvaged by divers.

It wasn't only enemy aircraft that posed a danger to the public. Flying was still not an exact science, as was shown in Twickenham when a British aircraft crashed into the roof of a house, causing quite severe damage to the building. The pilot and the occupants of the house were unhurt.

One of the pilots who was to fly against the bombers was Cecil Lewis, who was sent home from France wounded and then posted to 44 Squadron at Hainault Farm. The squadron was equipped with Sopwith Camels, each of which had a 110hp engine and two Vickers guns. Although based at Hainault, according to Lewis most pilots spent their nights in London. This seems to detract from the idea of rapid defence against raids if the pilots were miles from the base.

There was by this time an advanced warning system for air raids. Messages could come from as far away as Holland and then from ships in the North Sea and lightships in the Thames Estuary. They would telephone the Home Defence HQ at Horse Guards. The message would then be passed on to all Home Defence squadrons.

There were two rings of defence – an outer and an inner. The outer ring was based around Southend, where aircraft were based. Then there was the area in-between, which was full of anti-aircraft guns and balloons, which, it was hoped, would catch bombers with their cables. The inner ring was from Epping in the north to Kenley in the south.

A raid would be announced with klaxons and all the aircraft would scramble and take off. When the raids changed to night-time there was a problem, as very few pilots had flown at night.

A squadron that had been sent back from France for home defence, 46 Squadron, was wanted back at the front. Sir Douglas Haig wrote to the War Cabinet at the end of August requesting that the squadron be returned to France. The first sea lord had apparently informed Haig that some RNAS squadrons in France needed maintenance.

Haig claimed that increased air activity by the enemy on the front, combined with the decreased strength of the RNAS squadrons, rendered it essential that the air force of the army in France be strengthened at the earliest opportunity. Haig called for the immediate replacement of No. 10 RNAS Squadron by No. 46 Squadron RFC.

He also asked that the pilots and aircraft of No. 10 Squadron RNAS be transferred to other RNAS squadrons to increase their strength; a second RNAS squadron be replaced by No. 84 Squadron RFC, which was due to arrive in September; and a third RNAS squadron be replaced by Nos. 64 or 28 Squadron RFC as soon as they could be sent to France. The two remaining RNAS squadrons should be maintained in France until November.

The Air Board reported to the Cabinet in August that they were to order 700 long-distance bombing machines. These were the de Havilland 9, described as a fast machine with a speed of 112 miles per hour at 10,000 feet but only carried 460lbs of bombs, with a range of 450 miles.

The board had been considering for some time supplementing the light bombers with a number of heavy bombers. The twin-engined Handley Page type carried 3,000lbs of bombs, which was six times the de Havilland's load. It was, however, much slower, at only 83 miles per hour. The larger aircraft were mainly used for night bombing. Although this would seem to make the larger aircraft less effective, the RNAS had been using them with great success and not one of them had been brought down by the enemy.

The board therefore decided to supplement the light bomber order with one for 100 Handley Page bombers. The report also gave aircraft production numbers for June 1917 as 1,178 engines, 1,081 aeroplanes and forty-nine

The Handley Page Heyford long-range bomber. A rival for the German Gotha.

seaplanes. This compared well with June 1916, when there were 335 engines, 441 aeroplanes and no seaplanes.

The report also included a letter to Colonel Raynal Bolling of the American Air Service. It was concerned with the delivery of silver spruce (timber ideal for use in aircraft because of its strength to weight ratio) but also went on to express concern over the fact that the Americans were ordering aircraft engines from France. This is something of a surprise when one considers the resources available to the Americans and that much of the raw materials for production came from America. The Air Board were concerned that the American orders would interfere with the British orders for French engines.

The Air Board letter stated that the French producers of Hispano-Suiza engines needed to supply 400 engines per month to Britain before any could be supplied to America. There were also orders for engines for the Russians and the French Government so it seemed unlikely that they could also supply the Americans. There was also an order for 1,000 Le Rhone engines from France, but the first 500 were to go to Britain the next 500 to America.

By September there had been further concentration in the type of machines in use by the flying services. There were by this time only thirteen different engine types in use and only fourteen different aircraft, although there were other new aircraft in the process of production. There were also attempts to concentrate production in larger works rather than in so many small factories so the government decided to open three National Aircraft Factories, each capable of producing 200 machines per month.

There were still problems securing the materials needed for building aircraft. One of these materials was silver spruce, which the government had believed was to be a priority for supply to Britain from the Americans. At a conference with Colonel Bolling, the chief American aviation officer in Paris, it was agreed that Britain would receive fifty per cent of the spruce available for export from America for the rest of the year. Thirty per cent would go to France and the rest to Italy.

Aircraft engines were still being supplied to Britain by the French in large numbers. They promised 750 110hp Le Rhone engines by the end of the year for training aircraft and 150 Hispano-Suiza engines immediately.

Materials were a problem, but so were those employed to turn the materials into aircraft. As well as the different organizations competing against each other to control this, there were also some who wanted to be involved in more than one aspect of the argument. The secretary of the National Service Committee wrote to the War Cabinet in September. The letter regarded the formation of a committee to look into the conditions prevailing in the manufacture of aircraft and whether any priority should be granted. It went on to argue that priority of materials would be no good without priority of labour. As the committee would have recommendations regarding the allocation of manpower it was suggested that the Minister of National Service should be a member of the committee.

There was also a communication from Douglas Haig in September concerning the proposed Air Ministry. He saw the plans as a move from two authorities, the Admiralty and the Army, to one with three authorities, the third being the Air Ministry. As there had been little agreement so far between the first two, he asked if the new system would be any better when it had proved impossible up until now.

Cecil Lewis was transferred to Rochford with 61 Squadron. There was also a training squadron based at the airfield. They had Sopwith Pups but then changed to SE5s. One night, a Gotha landed at Rochford with engine trouble and crashed into a tree. The crew were taken prisoner and, unfortunately, the aircraft was accidentally set on fire and destroyed before it could be examined. The Gotha crew were transported up to London by train. News had got out and there were crowds at every station on the way to abuse the 'baby killers'.

The Gotha wasn't the only plane to crash at Rochford. One of the planes based there crashed into the ground, killing the pilot, and two others collided with fatal consequences for the pilots.

There was still little in the way of warning of approaching raids for the public and few shelters to run to if there was. The discussions about air raid warnings seemed to be ongoing. One form of warning was a car driven by special constables with a 'take cover' sign on the front. This would be driven around the streets but did little to warn anyone who was inside, and meant that the driver was forced to stay in the open during raids. The car could also carry 'all clear' signs to display after the raid had ended.

At a meeting of the War Cabinet on 15 October, the formation of an air ministry was again discussed. This was due to public interest and a question to be asked in Parliament in regard to the aerial situation. The Cabinet invited General Smuts to make a statement as to the progress of the recommendations made the previous month to appoint a committee to investigate the amalgamation of the RFC and the RNAS and the relationship between it and the War Office.

General Smuts reported that his committee had already covered a great deal of ground. A bill had been prepared giving the powers to form a new air service. They had also drawn up an order for the formation of an air council, whose functions would correspond to those of the Army Council and the Board of the Admiralty.

A great deal of detail still had to be worked out so it was decided that it was advisable at that time only to inform Parliament that a bill was in the process of being prepared. The Secretary of State for War said that he had not yet seen the bill and that it could not be introduced until its provisions had been closely examined by the Admiralty and the Army.

Despite the bill it seemed that General Smuts still did not think that an air ministry could be introduced during the course of the war. There was, therefore, an immediate question as to how the air services could be best co-ordinated during the conflict – a question that had been under discussion for a number of years by this time. General Smuts said that if the War Cabinet agreed with him that creating an air ministry was not possible at the present time then some interim arrangement may be introduced during the war. This could be a small Cabinet committee responsible for the direction of air policy. The Air Board had no power over policy; it was just a supply department.

Lord Cowdray agreed that the Air Board had no policy apart from the supply of aircraft. He had foreseen, however, a surplus in aircraft being available, which could then involve the Air Board being granted greater powers. He asked for a general staff to decide if the surplus was being used correctly.

The War Cabinet decided that only the Cabinet or someone appointed by them were competent to decide on air policy between the Admiralty and the War Office. It was decided that General Smuts would continue to supervise the air policy on behalf of the Cabinet.

It had seemed as if the Zeppelin was a thing of the past now that the raids were being carried out by Gothas. However, on 19 October, bombs began to fall on London without warning. The following day the newspapers reported that the attack had been carried out by a fleet of Zeppelins. It was only found out days afterwards that of the eleven airships that carried out the attack, six had been brought down in France as they returned home.

In October, the Home Secretary hosted a conference of local authorities on the subject of air raids. It was reported that there were now shelters available for one million people. The government had ruled that anyone possessing a shelter had to place it at the disposal of the public.

Recruits for the air services often came from other regiments. This recruiting poster for the Sportsman's Battalion shows how one of their members went on to fly.

The month of October was also to finally see movement towards the unification of the air services. A report in *The Times* on the 17th stated that the formation of an air ministry had been too long delayed and that there was now no serious opposition in Parliament to the idea. The report went on to state what had been obvious for some time: that the inevitable obstruction of vested interests had prevented its establishment for too long.

It seemed as if the conflict between the air services was to finally end in November, when the Air Force Bill received Royal Assent at the end of the month. General Smuts had called for a new air service on the same level as the Army and Navy. This was due to his belief in the possibility of the potential for the devastation of enemy lands on a vast scale by aircraft.

The end of November saw the success of what had been attempted for so long when Lord Rothermere became Air Minister, although it seems that the foundation of the Air Ministry was not the end of the matter. A report in *The*

The aircraft stores seem to have been run by civilians. It looks as though one of the employees has allowed his family in to experience being in an aircraft.

Times on 27 November stated that the new minister would from the outset be faced with difficulties of holding his own between the two older services. He was also faced with a serious shortage in the production of aircraft.

Early December saw a large attack, which came in waves. The first wave bombed around the Kent coast at around 1.15 am. At 3.00 am, another group flew up the Thames and over Kent. At 4.00 am, two more groups of planes flew towards London. It was thought that the plan was for all the groups of aircraft to attack London at the same time.

Only one group is reported to have actually reached the capital. The others were turned back by anti-aircraft fire. Two of the attacking aircraft were then shot down. One was captured intact with its bombs still on board.

These raids also included aircraft that were even larger than Gothas. The four-engined Giant planes had a 140-foot wing span and carried over 2,000lbs of bombs. In December, Captain G. Murkiss-Green, the commander of 44 Squadron from Hainault Farm, flying a Sopwith Camel, shot down a bomber.

Nineteen-eighteen

The beginning of the final year of the war was to see the most important step in the formation of an air service that was independent of both the Army and the Navy. Despite the need for such an organization for the previous four years, it was only now that the Air Ministry was finally formed.

A Cabinet meeting in January discussed the location of the new Air Ministry base. There had been a suggestion that the British Museum could be used. Then, of course, the arguments began involving those concerned with the museum and debating how long it would take to pack and remove the exhibits. The idea was soon abandoned.

The first Air Minister was to be Lord Rothermere. Rothermere was a well-known newspaper proprietor and controlled the *Daily Mail* and the *Daily Mirror*. The Air Council was made up of men who had played a part in the air services. Lieutenant General Sir David Henderson was Vice President, Major General Sir Hugh Trenchard was Chief of Air Staff and Major General Godfrey Paine was Master General of Personnel.

The ministry originally met in the Hotel Cecil on the Thames Embankment. The Cecil had once been the largest hotel in Europe. At the beginning of the war it had been used as an upmarket recruiting office for the Sportsman's Battalion, a special battalion made up of personalities from the world of sport and entertainment.

When an attack on London took place on 28 January, it didn't go well for all the enemy aircraft. Two British planes came across the bombers as they crossed Essex and shot down one of them; all the crew died. The two victorious pilots were Captain Hackwill and Lieutenant Banks, both of the RFC.

The news of the success was given by Viscount French as Officer Commander-in-Chief of the Home Forces. He said that a number of RFC machines went up to meet the raiders. The battle took place at 10,000 feet, the Gotha bursting into flames and plunging towards the ground, giving the crew no chance of survival.

The Times published an article on 16 March with the title of 'The Royal Air Force'. It stated that an air force would be raised consisting of such numbers of officers and men decided by Parliament and to be called the Royal Air Force (RAF).

A report in *The Illustrated War News* in March revealed how the most modern form of war machine, the aircraft, often relied on more historic forms of support. It was reported that all seaplanes carried two carrier pigeons. In the event of a problem such as the machine coming down in the sea, the pigeons could be sent off with messages giving the position from where the aircraft could then be rescued.

Following the announcement of the formation of the RAF it was declared a few weeks later that a women's RAF would also be formed. The new service would be known as the Penguins and it would be commanded by Lady Gertrude Crawford. It would be similar to the WAAC (Women's Auxiliary Army Corps) and the WRNS (Women's Royal Navy Service). The recruits would live in hostels at the bases to which they were sent.

The first day of April was to finally see the amalgamation of the two air services when the RAF was formed under the control of the Air Ministry. It was the world's first air force independent of an army and navy. The RFC squadron numbers were kept as they were, while the RNAS squadrons were numbered from 201.

The Times published an article on 1 April stating:

Today, the Royal Naval Air Service and the Royal Flying Corps become the Royal Air Force. The old system was an improvisation from the days when the flying man was seen as no more than an accessory. This led to a duplication of personnel, construction and requisitions.

Despite the increasing success of pilots against airships, they were still being used for raids. In April 1918, the third airship raid of the year took place when five airships attacked. There were seven killed and twenty injured during the bombing. The Germans had also begun to use seaplanes to capture merchant vessels. They would land by the vessel and put an observer from the aircraft on-board the ship. The aircraft would then escort the ship into an enemy port.

Considering the lack of searchlights early in the war, things had changed greatly by this time. The early searchlights were almost entirely used in anti aircraft pursuits. By this time, however, there were also numerous other lights around the coast that not only searched the skies at night but also the waters around the coast for enemy ships.

Those in command of the lights were normally officers or warrant officers and were often engineers. They would have a group of men under them

The London Stores Distribution Park, now the RAF. The women are members of the Women's RAF.

who were responsible for keeping the lights in good order. This included the machines that supplied the power for the lights. While a light was in use, one man would always be watching the arcs through a special window in the mechanism; no matter what the beam may have been trained on, his job was to watch his own objective.

Despite some success by the defenders, more of the German bombing aircraft were destroyed by collisions and landing accidents than by the RFC. The last raid on London took place in May 1918. It involved more than forty aircraft and was met by more than eighty fighter planes. Three of the German planes were shot down by aircraft and three by anti-aircraft fire.

The formation of the Air Ministry and the amalgamation of the two air services into the RAF did not solve all the problems with air policy straight away. A memo from the new Air Minister to the War Cabinet in May revealed this. He stated that his belief was that the ministry should be devoted to the interruption of the German war effort by long-range bombing. He went on to argue that long-range bombing was purely an aerial operation whereas seaplanes and torpedo-carrying aircraft and aircraft based on ships had a naval connection. It was with bombing that the ministry seemed to be most concerned.

Due to this concentration on long-range bombing it was decided to appoint General Trenchard as the commander of the Long Range Bombing Group. It would seem that rather than unifying the air services, they had been divided even further. There were at the time only four bomber squadrons; one was still incomplete. It was hoped to bring this up to twenty-four squadrons by October.

Once up to full strength, the force would be capable of continuously bombing Germany. It was thought that France would not agree with this, due to the chance of German retaliation on French cities.

The memo also went on to state that whatever the requirements of the Navy and Army, decisions as to their fulfilment must be made by the ministry. This was to be especially true if the available resources fell below the demands of the air services.

Airmen did not only die during the war. Fatalities continued after the war ended, as this gravestone from Hornchurch churchyard shows.

Airships were still being used up to the last few months of the war. The last airship raid took place in early August and five Zeppelins were involved. The *L70* was shot down by Cadbury and Leckie from Great Yarmouth. They thought they had shot down the *L65* as well, but it made it home. The *L53* was shot down by a Sopwith Camel launched from a lighter being towed by the Harwich Force. The pilot, Lieutenant Culley, landed afterwards and was picked up.

In October, Winston Churchill raised the question of what was to happen to the Ministry of Munitions once the war had ended. He gave two alternatives: the ministry should come to an end at the conclusion of the war and its elements be dispersed; or a ministry of national supply should be set up to continue to permanently supply materials needed by the Army.

Part of the problem was to be the disposal of the national factories set up for producing war materials. Included in this were the National Aircraft Factories. It was stated in the report on the work of the Munitions Council Committee dealing with the problem of national factories that, in relation to the aircraft factories, many of them were only in the course of erection at the time of the report. It was stated that some may be retained as national establishments. There were also some factories whose status was not determined as they were owned by the government but were managed by private firms.

Chapter 4

The War in Europe

Nineteen-fourteen

There were varying opinions as to how aviation would affect the war when it first began. An article published in *The War Illustrated* magazine written by the well-known figure in aviation, Claude Grahame-White, stated that military aircraft at the start of the war were destined for five uses in the conflict but at the time were only efficient in two of these. These were in their use as scouts and in directing artillery fire.

There were, however, no fighting aircraft that were armoured, no aircraft that were able to attack fortified enemy positions, or any capable of carrying troops to enable them to be quickly deployed. According to Grahame-White, the war came five years too soon.

General Joffre, chief of the French General Staff, inspecting a German Albatross that had just been brought down.

When the war began in Europe there were only four squadrons of the Royal Flying Corps ready to cross the Channel. They flew down to the south-east and were based around Dover, from where they would take off for France. There was, of course, a danger of the aircraft not making it across the Channel and ships carrying troops and equipment had been warned to watch out for aircraft ditching in the sea.

The first to cross was No. 2 Squadron led by Major Charles Burke, previously of the Royal Irish Regiment. The squadron flew BE2as. Some pilots carried a mechanic in the observer seat. The rest of the squadron's members travelled across by ship. Some never managed the crossing and Lieutenant Robert Skene, pilot, and Raymond Barber, mechanic, of No. 3 Squadron, crashed and became the RFC's first casualties of the war. No. 3 Squadron had a mixture of BE2s and BE8s.

To get across the Channel safely the aircraft had to reach a height of 3,000 feet. Then, if their engine broke down, they would hopefully be high enough to glide the rest of the way across. When they reached Boulogne they had to fly along the coast to the Somme Estuary, and then follow the river to the aerodrome at Amiens. There were few instruments to help the pilots find their way. Landmarks on the ground directed them. The first pilot to arrive was Harvey-Kelly. Once they had all arrived they then moved up to the forward base at Maubeuge.

The first men there had to get the airfield ready for those following. In those days this was not a very big job as aerodromes were quite basic. It often just involved clearing any large obstacles such as haystacks out of fields so that aircraft could land. One other task involved finding a piano for the mess, which seemed to be a necessity. Near the airfield at Maubeuge was a large shed holding two French airships.

The Germans had begun to use their airships for bombing early in the conflict. According to *The War Illustrated* magazine, one of the earliest instances of bombing during the war was when they bombed the royal palace in Belgium towards the end of August. The view of the action was critical. In international law, notice of bombardment of a city should have been given to enable non-combatants to find shelter. The bombing of civilians in war was something new. It would soon become clear that neither side were about to give notice of raids before they took place.

Early reports seem to state that although Zeppelins were useful for destroying civilian sites, they were much less use against military targets that could fire back. Whether this was correct is doubtful, as can be seen from the difficulty there was in destroying the large airships that began to bomb England a few months later.

The early days at war were difficult for the RFC. The only weapons the aircrafts carried were rifles and revolvers. They were often shot at by Allied troops who mistook any aircraft for an enemy. Union flags were painted on the bottom of the wings but this didn't help as they were then mistaken for the crosses on German aircraft.

The first flights for reconnaissance began in late August. Lieutenant N. Noel was piloting the first plane to be hit, and his passenger, W. Jellings of No. 2 Squadron, was the first man to be wounded in the air.

According to Sir John French's dispatch of 11 September, the RFC had been very successful in the collection of information. Up to 10 September, a daily average of around nine reconnaissance flights had been maintained to locate the positions of enemy forces.

The best early example took place at Mons, when airmen confirmed that there were three German corps threatening the British front while another attempted to turn its flank. Airmen confirmed the situation within an hour, a task that would have taken cavalry scouts at least a day.

The pilots also carried three bombs for use against Zeppelins. One of the first bombing raids by the British was made on 23 September, when

The Avro 504J with a 100hp Gnome Monosoupe engine. The 504 was one of the most numerously produced aircraft of the First World War.

Flight Lieutenant C.H. Collet flew over the Zeppelin sheds at Düsseldorf and dropped his three bombs. Despite his aircraft being hit by fire from the ground he made the 100-mile-plus trip back across Belgium to his base.

The main use of the aircraft in the early stages of the war was almost entirely for reconnaissance. What the early pilots saw were mainly German advances and they found themselves retreating along with ground forces. After the Battle of Mons they moved back to Le Cateau, then again to St Quentin as the German Army advanced towards Paris. The pilots tried to help the infantry by dropping grenades on the advancing Germans but were still forced to move again to Le Fene, and then to Compiègne.

The early attacks on enemy troops were not very successful, as the aircraft did not have the weapons to cause much damage to troops on the ground. What they did achieve was damage to enemy morale. Attacks on larger targets such as Zeppelin sheds were more successful, as the targets were much bigger and could be hit by bombs.

There were often no troops available to guard the RFC force until a unit of the Northern Irish Horse and some French territorials arrived in September. How strange that an ancient part of the Army, the cavalry, should be used to guard the most modern part of the forces.

A German airfield with aircraft ready to take off.

The German advance was finally held and the change from large-scale movements to static trench warfare soon became the norm. Before the trenches stretched from the sea to Switzerland, it was easy for German troops to infiltrate the Allied areas. One group of supposedly Belgian officers, who were found at Villers-Cotterets, near the aerodrome, turned out to be German, and were shot.

The RFC were, by early October, based at St Omer. They flew two flights a day, often below 1,000 feet so they could see what was happening on the ground. Kitchener was planning for fifty squadrons of aircraft, which seemed unbelievable at the time. Where were the machines and the pilots to come from?

Anti-aircraft fire was more precise now that those firing the guns had some practice, and the aircraft were slow enough to be hit from the ground. They were still just as often hit by friendly fire. It was then decided to paint roundels on the aircraft similar to the ones the French had on their aircraft, but in British colours.

There was one unusual operation that was undertaken by the RFC early in the conflict. Instead of just watching the Germans on the ground, they tried to kill one of them. The kaiser was on a trip to the front. There were attempts to bomb the area he was visiting but it seems he had already left before the aircraft arrived on the scene.

Many of the early attempts at aerial warfare were cases of making the best of equipment that did not really match up to the job. Trucks were used to store the small bombs that the pilots used to drop from the air. Someone threw a bomb at one of the trucks, the resulting explosion wounding five men and killing one. It was never discovered who threw the bomb.

Bristol Scout aircraft were soon arriving in France and were faster than the earlier aircraft, but having only a single seat made it difficult for the pilot to fly the plane and fire a weapon at the same time. Radio telegraph equipment also began to be used in aircraft but, because of the weight of the telegraph, two-seater aircraft could then only carry one man and the telegraph. This made it even more difficult for a pilot who had to fly *and* send messages.

Early in the war, aerial photography was also being used to map German defences. Again, the equipment for this was difficult to use as the pilot only had a hand-held camera. To add to their problems the Germans had developed a firing system for the Fokker Eindecker, which allowed them to fire machine guns through the propeller. Fortunately, the aircraft that could do this were not available in large numbers.

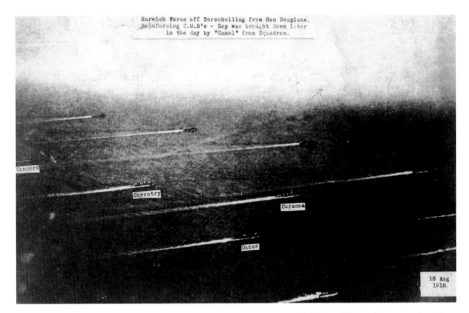

Aerial photography was in its infancy during the First World War. This photograph, taken from a German seaplane, shows the Harwich Force of destroyers off Terschelling, an island in the northern Netherlands.

There were often visits to the RFC headquarters by celebrities of the period. Hilaire Belloc, the well-known writer, visited in November and came back on a number of other occasions. Someone asked him why the press abused the Germans so badly. It seems that those doing the fighting had more respect for the enemy than those at home did.

The RNAS were active in bombing raids early in the war and in November three airmen made the 120-mile trip to bomb the Zeppelin workshops at Friedrichshafen. The men were Squadron Commander E.F. Briggs, Flight Commander J.T. Babington and Flight Lieutenant S.V. Snipe.

The Germans defending the base had been informed by telegraph of the approach of the aircraft and were able to greet them with a great deal of anti-aircraft fire. Briggs was hit and had to land but still dropped his bombs as he flew down. He was wounded and taken prisoner.

The other two aircraft made it back to base and reported that a Zeppelin and a shed had definitely been destroyed by the bombing. The Germans denied that this was the case. Conflicting views from both sides of such events were common throughout the war.

GUERRE 1914/15
Védrines partant en reconnaissance sur son appareil qu'il a surnommé "La Vache"

A French reconnaissance flight about to take off in an aircraft nicknamed *The Cow*.

The first Christmas Day of the war was to see a joint force involving aircraft, warships and submarines make a bombing attack on Cuxhaven submarine base. Seven RNAS aircraft took part in the raid. Two German airships were supposed to be protecting the German base but fled when attacked.

Nineteen-fifteen

In February 1915, the first Voisin arrived at St Omer. Bombing was often practised on the RFC's own airfields first before being attempted on the enemy. One early bombing success was the attack on railway lines behind the German lines before the attack on Neuve Chapelle in March 1915. Later attempts were not as successful, until a bombsight was developed by the Central Flying School in mid-1915.

A new recruit arrived at St Omer in March as an observer. No one could have known at that time what an influence William Leefe Robinson was to have on the war in the air. Robinson joined No. 4 Squadron.

Observers had just begun to use the clock system to report the accuracy of artillery fire. The target would be at the centre of a clock marked on the map

A postcard showing the form of modern warfare taking place in Europe, with ships aircraft and air ships

with lettered rings radiating outwards. This enabled the observer to send details to the ground as to where the aim of the artillery should be adjusted.

Robinson's excitement in his new role was to be short-lived. He was wounded by shrapnel and was sent home to England in May. What his short spell as an observer had done was to awaken a love of flying that was to lead to his qualification as a pilot.

According to Captain Baring, who was on General Trenchard's staff at his Flying Corps Headquarters and recorded his experiences of the First World War in his book *Royal Flying Corps HQ 1914-1918* (first edition 1920), the artillery were far from happy with the early attempts at co-operation between them and the RFC. He put this down to a refusal to accept anything new in war.

One of the amazing flying stories of the war took place on 7 June when Flight Sub-Lieutenant Warneford RNAS was flying his Morane Saulnier Type L over Ghent. He came across the German airship *LZ37*. He dropped his bombs on the airship, causing it to explode. The explosion, however, caused Warneford's aircraft to turn over, which supposedly caused the petrol to run out of the tank, forcing him to land in enemy territory.

Warneford managed to refill the tank, get his engine started and then flew back to base. Although he survived the effects of the exploding airship, for which he received the Victoria Cross, he was killed a few days later while flying an American reporter on a test flight. The plane's wings collapsed and both men were killed. Flying was still dangerous even when the enemy were absent.

By mid-1915, many of the British aircraft were carrying machine guns but these were usually fired by the observer in two-seater craft. Some firing systems were developed for single-seaters. These usually fired above the propeller but this meant that to change the drum on the gun, the pilot had to stand up and reload while still flying the plane.

Bombs were still not very stable by mid-1915, and a number of them that proved unsafe were destroyed by being thrown into a gravel pit. On 14 June at St Omer, one of the supposedly useless bombs exploded and set fire to the grass. The fire spread towards the bomb store. It needed all the men on the base to put it out before a disaster occurred.

The Germans added to the danger by bombing St Omer in July. On the first raid they also dropped a note stating that they would bomb the town every day for a week until it was destroyed, but they never carried out their threat. It must have been one of the only occasions during the war when either side revealed bombing intentions.

L. Howden arrived at St Omer in late 1915 as an observer. He was a member of No. 6 Squadron, who were flying FE2bs. They later had RE8s, which they called Harry Tates. To fire backwards, Howden had to stand on the seat and so was not strapped in. He said that a lot of observers fell out of their aircraft during dogfights. He also said that every three weeks, observers had to spend a week in the trenches decoding Morse code messages from artillery spotters.

Captain Baring was sent to Italy late in 1915 to look at a Caproni aircraft. The commander of Italian aviation, General Morris, told him that although this might be unbelievable to an Englishman, there was some level of conflict between the Italian military and naval aviation forces. Baring seemed to find it amusing that the general did not think that this was also true of aviation in Britain. This was, in fact, to become one of the most serious problems relating to air policy throughout the conflict.

A postcard showing a crashed British aircraft, possibly a BE2c, being examined by German officers.

By August there were three wings in France, each with various numbers of squadrons. The only aircraft park was at St Omer. General Trenchard had the idea of forming a park for each of the three wings.

By late 1915, there were 160 aircraft spread over twelve squadrons. They were mainly BE2cs and Morane Parasols. The BE2cs became known as Fokker fodder. The German Fokker was a copy of the French Morane. By 1916, the new DH2 was arriving and it was hoped that it would be a more equal match for the Fokker.

There was a report in the newspapers of the capture of two German aircraft in October. One was a new type of Albatross. The two crew members of the aircraft gave an account of how they were forced to land and be captured. They said they were attacked by anti-aircraft fire and four British aircraft. One shell supposedly almost capsized the German machine. The aircraft then manoeuvred to each side of them to force them to land. The Germans were only armed with a carbine; there were no machine-gun mountings on the aircraft.

The German machine, however, showed little sign of being attacked. There were only two bullet holes in the fuselage just behind the second crewman's seat. The pilots who drove the German down said that the aircraft had not been handled well. The Albatross came to ground very quickly after it had been fired on.

The second machine, an Aviatik, did put up more of a fight. It was pursued by seven British fighters and managed to lose all but one of them. This one then drove the German back towards the other British craft. The German observer was badly wounded in the battle.

There were often problems with new aircraft that had a tendency to spin, and this led to a number of crashes. There were still more fatalities occurring in flight training than in action at the front. Most new pilots were very young and inexperienced. Some arrived at the front with the number of flying hours they had experienced in single figures. The supposed continued training at the front often did not happen and young, inexperienced pilots were sent off into action for which they were not ready.

There were undoubted problems with the stress of flying constantly but those involved in medicine were beginning to look deeper into the effects. An article in *The Lancet* in December 1915 discussed the effects of mountain sickness caused by thin air and the similarity to flying sickness.

In the article Edward Whymper described the symptoms as profound lassitude, intense headache, feverishness, accelerated respiration and

The Avro 504K was a modified type of the 504J. This was to take various different engines due to the shortage of engines at the time. This model has a 130 horse power Clerget.

occasional spasmodic gulping of air. It could also cause palpitations and tinnitus. Perhaps the feelings experienced by pilots were due to this rather than the stress of being constantly in danger.

Other symptoms experienced by men in war were being given medical explanations. Where soldiers had previously been executed for cowardice, it was now being understood that their behaviour could be due to shell shock, which was beyond their control, and that the effects of flying could produce similar symptoms.

Nineteen-sixteen

By 1916, the RNAS had fighter squadrons and light bombers operating on the Continent. The bombers mainly concentrated on the coastal areas, bombing the docks and enemy shipping, while the fighters were operating with the RFC on the front lines.

In March, Cecil Lewis was posted to France. He was just eighteen and went first to Rouen and then on to No. 22 Squadron at St Omer. This was the number one aircraft depot, from where all aircraft were sent on their way to the front. It was also the headquarters of the commander, General Trenchard.

Lewis described some of the conditions for pilots at the front. He said that pilots often got lost and landed to ask directions. At one point a Fokker was captured when a German pilot landed on a British airfield thinking he was on the German side of the lines. This was supposed to have happened to a British pilot as well. He also described how pilots could actually see British shells flying through the air as they watched over German artillery.

Lewis described how some of the aircraft operated. The BE2c was a two-seater with the observer in the front seat, from where he could see little. The observer could not fire the gun very well because the propeller at the front and wing struts obscured his view. Lewis said that the Morane was dangerous to fly but was a good aircraft for experienced pilots.

In April, a Fokker landed at Renescure, in northern France. The German pilot had got lost and had run out of fuel. The aircraft was taken to St Omer, where on close examination it was seen to be a copy of the Morane. One of the developments that the RFC copied from the captured aircraft was the metal links that were used to join ammunition together. These were much more use than the old-style ammunition belts.

A crashed British aircraft, possibly a Moraine Bullet, being examined by German officers and men.

Captain Baring mentioned that General Trenchard ordered Morane Bullet monoplanes for No. 60 Squadron on the advice of the pilots but against his better judgement. The aircraft were very fast but had poor visibility. They were the most expensive machines in terms of pilot lives. The Moranes eventually had to be taken out of service for some time.

German airships continued to be shot down and, in May, the *L7* was shot down off the German coast by the cruisers *Galatea* and *Phaeton*. After the Zeppelin came down a British submarine surfaced and completed the destruction of the airship with gunfire. The submarine picked up seven of the airship's crew but was driven off by a German cruiser and dived after being attacked.

By the time of the approach of the Battle of the Somme the RFC had gained ground on the Germans in both flying skills and aircraft design.

Captain and Flight Commander Albert Ball DSO. Ball was one of Britain's best-known and most successful fighter aces.

They had their own aces who had begun to make a name for themselves, such as Albert Ball.

Ball was a member of the Sherwood Foresters and RFC. He had been awarded the Military Cross, DSO and bar. He supposedly once attacked twelve German aircraft single-handed, firing a drum of ammunition into one that went down. He then fired three more drums at them, destroying another enemy machine before flying home with his own aircraft severely damaged.

He had no previous experience of flying before 1916. His favourite form of attack was to come up beneath his enemy and fire a drum of ammunition into him. He had a number of narrow escapes but had up to this point never been injured.

June 1916 was to see the arrival of the only three-winged fighter used by the British in the war. The Sopwith Triplane Scout had been trialled at Chingford and was taken up by the RNAS, who had used Sopwiths for some time. Production of the Triplane began from mid-1916. It was well received by Roderick Dallas, an Australian flying for the RNAS. This led to further orders for the aircraft, which was then supplied to a number of the RNAS squadrons in France.

The best known German ace of the early war was – Max Immelmann, famous for the Immelmann turn, a manoeuvre that could put him in a superior position during a dogfight. Immelmann had seventeen kills to his name. He was shot down and died in June 1916. The trouble with having well-known aces was that when they did die, it damaged morale. The Germans therefore blamed his death on machine failure rather than on having been shot down by the enemy.

He was, in fact, shot down by Second Lieutenant McCubbin, a South African. McCubbin had joined the RFC as a mechanic but then trained as a pilot. On 18 June, he saw two Fokkers shoot down and kill his friend, Lieutenant Savage. Immelmann was then shot down by McCubbin's observer, Corporal Waller. McCubbin was awarded a DSO and Waller was promoted to sergeant; observers were rarely awarded medals.

By the time of the Battle of the Somme, Cecil Lewis was with No. 3 Squadron flying Moranes at La Houssaye. During the bombardment before the battle they had to fly low under the clouds. They were told to attack enemy balloons but there were rumours that some of the balloons were decoys loaded with explosives. They used their guns or electrically fired rockets to destroy the targets.

Although the British had made advances in aerial combat, so had the Germans, and by the middle of 1916 a new German ace was beginning to build his reputation – Baron von Richthofen, the Red Baron.

As the battle of the Somme got underway the RFC tried to assist the troops on the ground, although this was not always possible. The infantry were supposed to light flares to show the pilots how far they had advanced. This also had the obvious effect of informing the enemy where they were, so it was often ignored.

There was a great deal of sympathy amongst the pilots for the troops on the ground. Many of them had transferred from infantry regiments. Some had even had experience of the trenches, although the airmen were much better off than the infantry. They were better housed and usually better fed. When not flying they also had plenty of free time.

When C. Bartlett arrived at a RNAS bombing squadron in August 1916, he said that it was normal for RFC pilots to go home after six months at the front. However, RNAS pilots stayed on the front line for as long as they could or as long as the medical officers would let them. They were using Caudrons for night bombing, and Sopwith 1½ Strutters with a bomb rack in the passenger seat for daytime bombing.

The Sopwith Bat Boat was the first successful flying boat in the years leading up to the war.

While bombing the coastal areas they were often subjected to what Bartlett called Flaming Onions. These were large green balls of flame fired up into the sky. He thought that they were possibly range-finding devices for anti-aircraft fire. They would take off on a mission around two hours before dawn. This meant that although it was still quite dark when they arrived at the target, they would land back at base in daylight.

The Illustrated War News published an article on the RFC in August. It explained how the airmen were finding new things to do. It stated that until recently they did little but scouting and dropping the odd bomb. Now they were more likely to attack troops on the ground with their machine guns, like a 'flying infantry'.

There was also a problem with slow spotter planes being destroyed by the faster German Fokkers. Spotting planes were now accompanied by fighter escorts to deal with the German fighters. According to the article, British and French fliers were able to overcome the enemy by such actions as looping the loop and coming to bear on the enemy's tail.

The article also explained how German observation balloons could be pulled down to the ground before they could be bombed, which had been the attackers' only option. They then began to destroy the balloons using an incendiary pistol before the balloon could be pulled down.

There was a personal account of a wounded pilot's flight back to base in *The Times* on 2 September 1916. The event had taken place on 2 August; the pilot wasn't named. He had dropped bombs on Marcoing, near Cambrai in France, and ran into an LVG German aircraft. He fired on it but then ran into a Roland – an adaptation to the Fokker that allowed shooting through the propeller. While firing on this aircraft he heard gunfire and found he was being pursued by three more Rolands. Then the pilot was hit in the leg but still drove the enemy machines off with his side gun. As well as being wounded there was also a hole in his petrol tank. The engine cut out and he began to glide down towards land. Using his left leg he blocked the hole in the petrol tank and began to pump the petrol. The engine started again at about 200 feet. He was still about 15 miles from the British lines at this point.

Although close to landing on several occasions, he managed to keep the engine running and covered the 15 miles at a height of around 50 feet. Being so low he was continually targeted by rifle and machine-gun fire from the ground. He eventually spotted a French aircraft and followed it. While trying to land behind the Frenchman, he crashed his aircraft but survived.

A RFC BE2c of No. 8 Squadron. It was brought down by Immelmann in March 1916. The crew of Lieutenant Grune and Second Lieutenant Glover were killed.

A number of bombing raids took place in August. Some of these were reported by the Air Board. On 2 August, nine aircraft bombed the Zeppelin sheds at Brussels. There were no direct hits on the sheds but some very close explosions. Heavy anti-aircraft fire was directed at the bombers, which had come down to 1,000 feet to drop their bombs, but all the aircraft arrived back safely. On the same day, another thirteen aircraft attacked Courtrai Station, on the river Leie in West Flanders. Direct hits were made on rolling stock, station buildings, the railway yard and the main line. There was heavy anti-aircraft fire and a number of German aircraft were engaged, but again, all the aircraft returned safely.

The following day, eight bombers and an escort attacked the Ronet railway sidings at Namur and the airship sheds at Cognelée, near Charleroi in Belgium. Only five of the aircraft reached the targets but did cause significant damage at both sites.

In September, General Trenchard wrote a memorandum that was then published as a pamphlet called 'Offence and Defence'. He stated that defensive measures to stop German aircraft crossing Allied lines were not possible. This was due to the unlimited space in the air and the difficulty of one aircraft spotting another. This was an obvious problem for the Home Defence squadrons, who could not stop the air raids. Trenchard argued that the aircraft was essentially an offensive and not a defensive weapon. Calls for defence were based on improving morale rather than a real effort to stop what damage attacks could do.

There was a report, in *The Times* in September 1916 regarding the part played in the Battle of the Somme by the RFC. An official communiqué stated how aeroplanes followed the British attacks and while flying low joined the battle using their machine guns on enemy troops. This was not the first time this had been done and many letters from men in the trenches mentioned how the enemy regarded the British airmen with terror.

According to the report German prisoners had less regard for their own airmen. They supposedly said that if an officer wanted to get fat he joined the Flying Corps, and then sat in the theatre in Lille with his breast covered in medals. Although this was obviously good propaganda the report did mention that this was unfair to the German airmen, who were held in high regard by the members of the RFC.

The RFC had an aura of glamour around it that made being a member something that men were proud of. As the war went on, there had also been a shift away from their early public schoolboy image. As high numbers of the original pilots were lost, replacements had to be found from Other Ranks, as well as from other countries when colonials became members.

Despite the fact that the war had been in progress for two years, there was still no clear process for supplying aircraft to the air services. A report to the government in September stated that the supply of aircraft material was the concern of two bodies, the War Office and the Admiralty, acting under the supervision of the Air Board. This process also involved competition with the Ministry of Munitions. It was suggested that the most satisfactory results would be to either hand the whole thing over to the Ministry of Munitions or set up a supply service to provide aircraft materials to both services.

The actual materials and means of production of the necessary items for the war were by this time in short supply. Placing all responsibility for the production of all the war materials in one place would have led to a more organized use of the production capabilities. Supplying surplus production in a market where materials fall short of demand was the problem that the Ministry of Munitions had been created to deal with. Control of production had been based on urgency, not profit, since the ministry had been formed.

In September, *The Illustrated War News* printed photographs of some Belgian aircraft with painted figureheads. One of these was said to be quite

A group of entertainers, some wearing RFC uniforms. Squadron No. 24 had entertainment groups called the Monos and the Joysticks. These may have been connected.

frightening, being the image of a Gorgon's head. The other was not quite as scary; it was a painting of Charlie Chaplin.

The report on the work of the RFC for September from Sir Douglas Haig raised some interesting points. One of these was that documents had been captured from behind German lines stating that the only way to defeat the English in the air was to follow their example and take to the offensive over their lines. Haig reported that the Germans were now doing this and, like British airmen, were flying low and attacking infantry.

Strangely, Haig went on to say that the one area where the Germans did lag behind was in bombing. They had done little night bombing and even less day bombing until the summer of 1917. This seems strange when one considers that the Germans had been bombing cities since early in the war. He argued that the raids that had been carried out by the Germans from 1917 were in retaliation for Allied raids on them. During September, the German bombing had been severe, especially along the coast. It had been the severest German bombing of the war so far.

Haig went on to say, however, that the Germans only bombed in good weather, while the British bombed day and night in all weathers and had therefore caused much more damage than the German attacks had. There were 226 raids carried out by the RFC, each consisting of six to twelve machines. The RNAS were not mentioned so they may perhaps have been included as RFC. In these raids, 7,886 bombs were dropped. The Germans, to the best of knowledge, had dropped ninety-six.

This seems to go against the idea that it was the Germans who did most of the bombing. There often seems to be an impression that it was the British who were responding to German raids with revenge attacks.

In regard to the number of enemy aircraft shot down, this was reported to have been 274 aircraft. Some of these were destroyed by anti-aircraft fire. In regard to this number, Haig mentions that valuable work was done by the naval squadrons attached to the RFC.

One of the little-known facts of First World War aviation history is the part played by women. A Mrs A.S. Hitchcock was operating an aircraft for

Early anti-aircraft guns were usually adaptations of what was available. This shows a Lewis gun fitted on a stand that allows it to be fired into the air.

the Italian Army during the war. A photograph of Mrs Hitchcock appeared in *The Illustrated War News* in October showing her explaining how to fire a Lewis gun from an aircraft. They also published a photograph of a Russian woman, Miss Peirse, who was flying for them and was the daughter of a Russian admiral.

When I looked into this further I found there were a number of women aviators. France had Hélène Dutrieu and Marie Marvingt. The Russians also had Princess Eugenie M. Shakhovskaya. They appear to have been mainly involved in reconnaissance; I have not come across any women who were participating in combat.

October saw another success for the Allies when Captain Boelke, the German ace with forty kills to his name, was killed. It seems that Boelke collided with another German aircraft during a fight. He managed to descend for much of the distance towards the ground before he lost control and his aircraft fell from the sky. He was honoured by British fliers who dropped a wreath in memory of him. After his death, a memorial service in his honour was held in Cambrai Cathedral, France.

In November, there was closer co-operation between the RFC and the RNAS. A naval squadron and RFC 32 Squadron shared an airfield. The naval squadron asked for military oil for their machine guns because naval oil was seen as not quite as good quality. The RFC, however, asked for naval oil as they believed that the military oil was not as good. It was found that there was no difference.

Also in November, Bron Lucas, as he was called by Captain Baring, died. He was actually Auberon Thomas Herbert, 9th Baron Lucas and 5th Lord Dingwall. The image of pilots during the war was of fit and healthy young men, which wasn't always true, as the baron proved. Lucas had fought in the Boer War and had lost a leg. He had become a Cabinet minister by the time the war began. After serving as an observer he trained as a fighter pilot and qualified. He died while flying, aged forty.

According to a report in *The Times* in early December, there had been some changes in the way air warfare on the Western Front was reported. German reports on aerial engagements had ceased halfway through the month, the last being made on the 11th. The report went on to say that of the few German reports made, none mentioned the date, time or location of the events. The article also commented that, since the death of Boelke at the end of October, the German Flying Service had appeared to become anonymous.

Reports from the Allied side were vague; although they sometimes gave numbers of machines brought down, they also on some occasions stated that many or several others were brought down. The report showed a table of aircraft lost for the past six months:

	British	**French**	**German**
June	7	28	37
July	48	31	86
August	26	42	121
September	48	68	206
October	42	25	104
November	32	4	112

There was no explanation as to why the number of German machines shot down had risen so quickly from August.

The fact that the RFC and RNAS were now bombing was common knowledge amongst the public and a report in *The Times* on 19 December

The Sopwith Triplane was very successful and used by the RNAS, but only in small numbers. This one was built by Oakley of Ilford. It was mainly replaced as the Sopwith Camel became more numerous.

A French seaplane about to take off from Dunkirk flying station.

described a number of bombing raids that took place in November. On the 14th, ten pilots carried out a series of raids. Railway stations and rolling stock were bombed, and two of the bombs hit a moving train. On 16 November, six aircraft bombed an enemy railway station. Six coaches were blown off the tracks, buildings were destroyed and other rolling stock damaged.

On 21 November, one RFC aircraft bombed and then machine-gunned a number of enemy lorries from a height of 150 feet. According to prisoners from German artillery units, a number of guns had been put out of action by air bombing.

Dunkirk was the base of a French seaplane flotilla. Several of the French seaplanes had joined British aircraft in bombing raids on Zeebrugge, Ghent and Bruges. It was one of the aircraft from Dunkirk that intercepted and shot down one of the German aircraft that had bombed London on 28 November.

Nineteen-seventeen

Early in 1917, the Germans began to venture over British lines more than they had done previously. This was probably because the aircraft they were flying were again superior to those that the British had. The only British plane that was comparable to the German aircraft was the Sopwith Pup.

It was in February that the RNAS squadrons in France began to be supplied with the Sopwith Triplane in quantity. Squadron Nos. 1, 8, 9 and 10 flew alongside the RFC. The new aircraft were well received by many of those who flew them. A number of the pilots flying for the naval flying force were by this time colonials.

Squadron No. 9 was formed in February and used the Nieuports and Sopwith Pups discarded by No. 8 Squadron. Their task was to protect the Channel ports and shipping, but they were also used as a reserve pool of pilots for the other naval squadrons until Squadron No. 12 was formed and took over this reserve role.

Despite the new aircraft arrivals, not everyone was happy with the number of aircraft being delivered to the front in France. Sir Douglas Haig wrote to the War Cabinet about the number of aircraft being delivered, which he felt was less than had been promised. The letter was forwarded to the Air Board.

The Air Board answered that the deficiency would be partly made good by squadrons lent by the RNAS and partly from aircraft with engines procured from France. No promise had apparently been given by the Director General of Military Aeronautics in regard to the missing aircraft. The information

The SE5a was an improvement on the SE5. It had a more powerful Hispano–Suiza engine.

that had been given to the commander-in-chief was, in fact, a forecast of dates that, at the time it appeared, would be when new squadrons would be available.

The forecast had perhaps been over optimistic and had not been realized because many of the aircraft had still been in the experimental stage, and some of these had been failures. Shortages were also due to the prevailing manufacturing conditions in the country. The War Cabinet was aware of this.

They went on to explain that the Air Board and Ministry of Munitions were gradually taking over the duties in connection with the design and supply of aircraft. The transfer would involve the amalgamation of some naval and military departments, which must be carried out with care and deliberation.

Further communication on the complaint was sent from the Army Council in February. It stated that two new squadrons and the replacements for three other squadrons that were promised in the previous September had not been available but now were. It also said that the replacements would from now be continuous, although would be dependent on the weather and the number of available ferry pilots.

A large German twin-engined aircraft.

The delivery of five squadrons that had been promised in September was late. One of these squadrons was to have been equipped with Sopwith two-seaters but by the desire of the General Officer in Command of the RFC, it had been withheld. It was to be supplied with different machines, which were due later. Of the remainder, three squadrons were due to leave in March, although two of these may have had only twelve aircraft.

Two RNAS squadrons had already been sent and another was due in March. The promise was that the deficiency in fighting squadrons would be made up by March. One replacement fighter squadron would be ready by the end of March. Two flights of another would also be ready by the end of the month and two more fighting squadrons had new machines fitted with engines from France.

In March, the RFC lost 120 aircraft; half of these were over the British lines. In April, high losses continued and it became clear that the new aircraft that were arriving still did not compare favourably to German machines. Delivery of those that were improvements on previous aircraft, such as the Bristol Fighter, SE5 and the Sopwith Camel, were being held up by strikes and labour disputes in the aircraft industry at home.

Because of the shortage of fast fighter aircraft, many of the artillery observer planes were being lost as they did not have enough escorts to keep the enemy aircraft away from them. The number of naval aircraft in France did go some way towards solving this problem but the Germans seemed to have the upper hand at the time.

By March, the first Handley Page bombers were beginning to arrive in France. They came from Manston in Kent, and usually had a crew of four. They were enormous aircraft that weighed 3½ tons when empty. When armed with bombs they weighed 5 tons and could fly for ten hours. As well as carrying bombs the aircraft were armed with three Lewis guns, and the early ones had two 250hp Rolls-Royce engines and carried fourteen 112lb bombs.

When pilots qualified they were supplied with a book of technical notes. This had information on all types of action that pilots undertook. It also had notes on all types of engines and many different aircraft, with diagrams of the machines. When W. Prothero was based at St Omer, his technical notebook, which is now in the Imperial War Museum, contained many personal jottings alongside the printed information. The book also stated that when requesting petrol from the stores the pilot had to say whether it was for an aircraft, car or motorbike.

The Handley Page bomber was one of the largest aircraft that the British had and could fly long-distance.

Cecil Lewis had spent some time back in England and was at London Colney with 56 Squadron. They had been supplied with SE5s with a 140hp Hispano-Suiza engine. They had two Lewis guns, one firing through the propeller and one on the wing firing above the propeller. This gun could be pulled down to reload and could then be fired straight upwards. They had been made by the Royal Aircraft Factory. They flew to St Omer in early April, and then on to Vert Galant, north of Amiens.

The squadron stayed in France until June, when they were sent back to England to deal with the menace of German bombers. Raids were not regular, however, and after two weeks they went back to France.

In April, Field Marshal Haig wrote to the Air Board stating that the difficulties of the air services were increased by the number of out of date machines they had to use and new types of machines that arrived too late in France for pilots to get used to them for the purpose of the offensive then in progress. Although the board agreed with the field marshal, they argued that the new squadrons that had been sent to France were flown by pilots who had been adequately trained in the aircrafts' use.

The reply from the board explained that the problem of new aircraft arriving late was mainly due to the delay in the production of new engines. New, more powerful, engines were needed for the increased demands

2-Engine Handley Page — wings folded for housing.

Fitting Handley Page bombers in hangars was difficult due to the restricted size of most hangars. Therefore, the wings were built to fold back.

of fighter aircraft, which had previously been mainly fitted with French engines. Now, due to the demands of their own air services, French engines were in very short supply. It had taken some time to begin to produce enough Rolls-Royce and Beardmore engines instead of French ones for the new aircraft.

Another problem with the Rolls-Royce engine was one that had plagued the RFC since the war had begun. Most of the Rolls-Royce engines had previously gone to the RNAS. This meant that very few of them were available to the RFC – another example of competition between the services. Added to this was the shortage of raw materials and labour.

Since the beginning of the year, the Air Board had been trying to impress on the Admiralty and the War Office that the present system of their competing for the supply of aircraft was detrimental to the public interest. Despite the appointment of Lord Derby to the Joint War Air Committee, the problem had still not been resolved.

By April, 48 Squadron did get Bristol Fighters. They were two-seater machines with the seats back to back. They had a Vickers machine gun in front and a Lewis gun at the rear. One of the pilots to fly these was Leefe Robinson, the man who had become a household name and had won the Victoria Cross for shooting down a Zeppelin.

Aircraft that had crashed always aroused interest. This German plane is being inspected by British troops.

Robinson had returned to France in March. Other pilots in France were not as impressed with his achievement as the public at home had been. They felt that shooting down a Zeppelin was not as dangerous a task as facing other aircraft. There had also been a number of others who had performed the same feat without achieving Robinson's level of fame.

Robinson was one of six pilots sent out in the new aircraft on 5 April to try and find the Red Baron. Unfortunately, they did just that. As a result, four of the six were shot down, including Robinson, who was then taken prisoner. He spent the rest of the war in various camps and prisons, often being mistreated by the Germans, who were well aware of who he was, which made him an easy target. The resulting effect on his health was thought to have led to his early death from Spanish flu after the war ended.

It seems that by this stage of the war some of the chivalry previously displayed by pilots was weakening. One pilot was fired on by a German aircraft after being shot down. It was also now more likely that the enemy would fire on an aircraft that was already damaged and on its way down.

The enemy didn't have it all their own way, however. Just as the sight of Richthofen's red aircraft would scare British pilots, the Germans were similarly scared of the red spinner on the propeller of the aircraft of Albert Ball, who was the leading British ace.

In April, RNAS No. 5 Squadron moved to Petite-Synthe, in northern France. They had supposedly been formed in December 1916, but it was April 1917 when Nos. 4 and 5 squadrons had parted company with four going to Bray Dunes. There they had been a mixture of fighters and bombers; No. 5 Squadron was now only made up of bombers. The Sopwith 1½ Strutters were by then slowly being replaced with de Havilland 4s. These had twin Lewis guns for the observer and twin Vickers guns that fired through the propeller for the pilot.

When Bartlett went back to England on leave he was given an aircraft to fly back with. It was a useful way of getting aircraft across to France as pilots were returning anyway. The plan was that he was to fly a Sopwith Pup from Brooklands. He had to land at Dover on the way because the aircraft was in a poor condition and the cockpit was full of oil fumes.

The effectiveness of aircraft attacking troops on the ground had improved by this period of the war. One such event was witnessed by a *Daily Mail* reporter in April. He reported that three British aircraft attacked Bavarian troops as they flew along the main street of Lens, in the Belgian province of Hainault. They flew at rooftop level and bombed the enemy, who retreated as fast as their legs could carry them. British troops reached the outskirts of the town shortly afterwards.

By the end of April the new aircraft were arriving in greater quantities and the imbalance between sides was becoming less marked. There were still problems when new pilots arrived in France, as they would often find themselves flying aircraft they had never used before.

Another view of a Handley Page bomber being prepared for flight.

May was to see a sad loss for the RFC. Albert Ball went missing, which was a severe blow to morale. He was later confirmed dead. Baring described Ball as the most modest and encouraging character.

In June there were several air raids at home carried out by German Gothas. To help combat this, two squadrons from France were sent to stop them. No. 56 Squadron was based at Bekesbourne, near Canterbury. Squadron 66 stayed in France and was based near Calais. This meant that both sides of the Dover Straits were covered against attack. After two weeks, the squadrons were recalled due to a lull in German raids and the bombing began again. This then led to reprisal bombing on German cities.

A report by the Air Board was made to the government in July. It stated that since its reconstruction at the beginning of the year it had been fully occupied with the problem of supplying enough aircraft to the two air services. Now that this had been achieved, the Air Board was to become involved in the mode of employment of the aircraft.

The War Cabinet had decided that a committee comprising the prime minister and General Smuts should consider the organization of aerial operations. The president of the Air Board would then lay before General Smuts his view arrived at in discussions that had taken place at the board. The opinion was that air policy should be decided by officers who were independent of the two air services. Those with responsibility for the

The Germans had their own long-range bomber, which could reach London – the Gotha.

Admiralty or War Office could not be depended on to offer impartial opinions – a fact that had plagued the air services since the war began.

There were several bombing raids on Gotha bases in September. Trying to destroy the enemy aircraft while on the ground was a better proposition than trying to catch them in the sky. The end of the month saw reprisal raids on Dunkirk by the Germans. On 29 September, a tavern by the cathedral was damaged and a car with a driver and two RFC officers was destroyed, killing the occupants. There were 125 deaths in the raids. A number of Allied planes were also destroyed in enemy raids, including those at Saint-Pol-sur-Ternoise, in northern France.

One of the most frightening parts of aerial combat was the possibility of an aircraft being damaged while at a great height. The thought of waiting to hit the ground as your plane fell from the sky must have been in the back of every pilot's mind. An even more worrying fear was if the aircraft caught fire. Despite this fear, there was still no progress on the supply of parachutes, even though a successful parachute jump had been made from a BE2c in January 1917 at Orford Ness. This was made by Captain Clive Collett, a New Zealander. What Collett used was a smaller than normal chute called the Guardian Angel.

Those in command had their own reasons for the lack of parachutes being supplied to pilots. There was supposedly no room for them in the cockpits. The extra weight was also a factor. Also, most fatalities actually occurred on taking off and landing, which the presence of parachutes would not affect. The biggest argument against them was that pilots would be more likely to jump out and save themselves than try to get home in a damaged machine.

There was some relief for British pilots in July, when Richthofen was wounded and put out of action for a while. At that time, the Germans were not getting things all their own way. The General of the German Fourth Army Air Service said in July that enemy fighters were appearing in overwhelming strength. This began to change as the Germans were being supplied with the new Fokker Triplanes. The German pilots would not only attack British aircraft, they also recorded any alteration or modification to the aircraft facing them.

The Allies were still gaining supremacy, however, and in August Richthofen's force was bombed on the ground at night; two hangars and seven aircraft were destroyed. When the Allies appeared over German lines flying at 4,000-5,000 feet, it was already too late for the German aircraft to take off. By the time the German aircraft were high enough, the Allied aircraft were already gone.

Lieutenant Adam, leader of German air squadron Jasta Six, wrote a description of a system of attacking British aircraft for his men. He said that when attacking Sopwith Camels or Pups they should attack from above towards either the front or rear. This could be carried out with no counter action from the Sopwiths. This was also how Se5s should be attacked. Adam believed that the Allied aircraft mentioned were inferior to the German Albatross D. All other Allied aircraft should be attacked from below but it was advisable to hit them with the first shot.

The Germans were not having everything their own way, however. Captain Guynemer, a French aviator, had just been made an officer of the Legion of Honour, which was not usually awarded to anyone under the rank of colonel. Not only was this unusual for a captain, Guynemer was, at twenty-two, already the youngest captain in the French Army. This was due to his remarkable record of forty-five kills, which included four German aircraft in one day and supposedly killing both a pilot and an observer in an Aviatik with only one bullet.

GENERAL PERSHING VISITS THE AVIATION CAMP AT LE BOURGET.

This postcard depicts General Pershing, the commander of the American Expeditionary Force, visiting Le Bourget Aerodrome, near Paris.

By late 1917 there was a serious shortage of observers and gunners. Although the pilots who flew in the war are generally remembered, the rest of the crew of the squadrons are mainly forgotten, including the observers, who often flew just as much as the pilots. Many of these passengers came from the infantry; it was a way of escaping from the trenches, although it was not an easy option. Usually, they received hardly any training and very few were ever decorated.

Some of the more experienced observers were used to train new pilots, whom they could direct with their experience. Many of them went on to train as pilots themselves. This also worked in reverse when some trainee pilots were tricked into becoming observers instead. If there was a shortage of observers, then some could fail their flying tests. It was useful for observers to have some flying experience and some two-seaters had a joystick in both cockpits so if a pilot was wounded or killed, an observer could bring the aircraft back to base.

Compared with the infantry in the trenches, however, the ground crew for the air services had quite an easy time. They did feel for the pilots, and had to put up with being bombed and attacked by German aircraft. At that time it was also their responsibility to protect the airfields. It had only been a recent development that German aircraft began to attack those on the ground, whereas the British had been doing this for some time in Germany.

A Gotha bomber was captured in France in August and was dismantled for examination. The results were far from secret as they were published in *The Illustrated War News* with a labelled diagram of the plane. It explained that the fore part was occupied by the gunner observer armed with a machine gun. The pilot sat behind the gunner in a separate compartment connected with a side passage. Behind this was a second gunner's compartment, which had all-round firing ability. The fuselage behind this was hollow, with a gun mounted in the floor. This was operated by the front gunner, who could move to the rear if the aircraft was attacked from behind.

August was not a good month for the British pilots. Richthofen returned, but his wound had not healed completely and he was soon on leave again. There was another German ace to worry about though, Werner Voss – a friend and rival of Richthofen who shot down his first two aircraft at the age of eighteen, and a total of forty-eight Allied aircraft, before being himself shot down and killed in September 1917 by Arthur Rhys Davids. Also of concern for British pilots in August, the new Fokker Triplane arrived in large numbers, giving the Germans air superiority again.

The Sopwith Snipe was intended as a replacement for the Camel. It only came into production at the end of the war. This model has a 230hp Bentley engine.

Although Richthofen may still not have been at his best, another member of his family was causing concern. Lothar Richthofen, the baron's brother, was also flying. He had managed twenty kills in his first four weeks of combat. The Germans credited his twenty-second kill as being that of Ball.

Some Allied pilots were also doing well, including one very young Canadian – Captain W.A. Bishop of the Canadian Cavalry and the RFC. He had shot down twenty-one enemy aircraft in his first fifty-seven flights. Included in this was an attack on an enemy aerodrome. He attacked the seven machines on the ground and shot down three that managed to take off. He was awarded the VC by the king. Bishop went on to play a major role in aviation in the Second World War. He was made an honourary air marshal in charge of recruitment in the Royal Canadian Air Force. He was so successful that they had to turn volunteers away. He then instigated a system of training for pilots until he retired due to ill health in 1944.

By late 1917, Handley Page bombers were based near Dunkirk and could carry fourteen 112lb bombs. Also, the SE5a had begun to arrive in larger numbers; it was a very good aircraft, especially when it had the Wolseley Viper engine fitted.

The French were using Breguet bombers, which were built to carry large weights and were huge aircraft. They had a two-man crew that sat well down inside the high fuselage. The bombers would often be accompanied by a Nieuport as protection against German aircraft.

The naval air base at Dunkirk was very busy in late August. A bombing raid took place on the Zeebrugge mole at 3.00 am on 22 August. At 6.30 am, another raid took place on Ghistelles aerodrome. All the aircraft returned safely from both raids. At 3.50 pm, four enemy scouts were attacked and two were driven down. There seemed to be two raids each night, as on the 23rd, Middlekerke and Raversijde Dumps were bombed at 2.00 am. At 7.00 am, Houttave Aerodrome was bombed. Again, all the aircraft involved returned safely.

In September, the war on the aircraft bombing England was taken to the Germans again. There were fifteen Gothas ready for flight at St Denis Westrem Aerodrome in northern Belgium; they were believed to be bound for a raid on London. They were discovered by a flight of the RNAS, who bombed the airfield, scoring one direct hit on a German aircraft and badly damaging the airfield. There were thirty-eight raids on German airfields by the RNAS during the month. This included six attacks on St Denis Westrem. The attackers often flew low enough to use machine guns on the personnel at the bases.

The RNAS also bombed German railheads, dumps and camps. This included the works at Bruges and the docks and factories of Ostend and Zeebrugge. It had also been promised that retaliation raids on Germany itself would happen as soon as possible. Some of the nearer German districts, such as Kaiserslautern and Saarbrücken, had already been bombed.

In a letter to the chief of the Imperial General Staff relating to the comments made by General Smuts, Sir Douglas Haig said, 'Bombing could lead to the devastation of enemy lands and destruction of industrial and population centres.' This was one of the reasons Smuts had used to justify the creation of an air force. Haig did not agree that there were no limits to the use of aircraft. Considering that he had experience of their limitations perhaps his opinion should have carried more weight.

Haig went on to suggest that officers with experience of long-distance bombing should be consulted as to its possibilities. He believed that the formation of an air ministry based on reasons that had no basis in fact was not a good idea. He also stated that the bombing of populous centres may be justifiable in order to punish the enemy for similar acts but that they had to morally outdo the enemy in this matter.

British aircraft waiting to leave for France.

Another aspect that Haig disagreed with was the calculation of a surplus of aircraft that would be available with the introduction of an air ministry. He argued that after three years of war and many broken promises there was still an acute shortage of aircraft. The proposed surplus had been based on figures quoted as needed fifteen months earlier.

The Illustrated War News published an article about the RFC in October. They pointed out that the common idea was that everyone in an RFC uniform that the public saw had his own aircraft and was constantly flying over German lines in it. This was of course far from being the case. The pilots and observers were, in their words, 'the high priests of a cult in which many thousands of Levites serve'. Of the many thousands of members of the RFC, only a few did or would ever fly. Many of the other RFC and RNAS members were master craftsmen. The fitters, turners and carpenters were responsible for the making and mending of the machines, a vital if less dangerous job than that of the fliers.

At the end of October, a raid took place into Germany and the steel works and railway station at Volkingen were damaged. There were direct hits on a furnace, a powerhouse and a train. The weather had been fine for the raid but snow and rain began to fall afterwards and one aircraft did not make it back.

There was also an unexpected raid on London in October by a fleet of eleven Zeppelins. It had been believed that the Zeppelin raids had finished. Perhaps it would have been better for the Germans if they had, because of the eleven airships that attacked London, six of them were later shot down over France as they returned home.

Of these, some fell victim to anti-aircraft fire and others to aircraft. One of these, the *L49*, was forced down by French aircraft. The crew got out and the commander began to fire his pistol into the balloon, hoping to destroy it. A French civilian, M. Jules Boiteux, who was out shooting, loaded his rifle and shouted at him to stop or he would fire. The commander of the airship and his eighteen crewmembers then surrendered. The fact that eighteen Germans had surrendered to one civilian was reported widely in Britain.

The *L49* was one of Germany's super Zeppelins. Being intact it was then available for examination by the French. The interior of the commander's cabin had the navigating controls in the fore part. The cabin contained a parachute for emergency escape. It also had a supply of oxygen and an eyepiece for aiming bombs.

In late October there was a meeting of the Air Policy Committee in Whitehall. When one considers that the war had by this time been underway for more than three years, it is difficult to believe that the main focus of the meeting were disputes about who was to command bombing and disagreement between the Army and Navy once again.

It seems that a decision by the committee at a meeting earlier in the month that aerial bombing operations on the Western Front should be under a separate air commander who would be under the command of the field marshal commander-in-chief in France had been ignored. It had also been decided that the first sea lord and Sir David Henderson should consult together to submit names to the committee to enable them to select an air commander.

Following these committee decisions the Army Council had written to Douglas Haig and implied that the commander of the bombing force should be a military officer. This then left the selection of names to Sir Douglas Haig. It was also decided that the second in command should be a naval officer whose name would be put forward by the Admiralty.

The Sopwith Swallow was an experimental Parasol built at the end of the war. It never went into production.

Sir Douglas Haig had argued that the officer commanding the RFC in France should be responsible to him for the operations of the whole flying forces in France. This would include working out long-term plans, including those for bombing. The officer appointed to command bombing would be given a free hand but still be under command of the officer in charge of the RFC. He then stated that if more RNAS service bombing squadrons were placed under his command he would be glad of the services of a naval commander as a wing or brigade commander.

At the same meeting there was a discussion about Handley Page bombers. The RNAS wanted another 100 of them while the Air Board had ordered 300. This could then mean that the output of machines would be larger than the number of available pilots to fly them. The committee discussed the possibility of training warrant and non-commissioned officers as bomber pilots. Larger machines were at that time only flown by officers. It was then pointed out that the pilots of large machines must have a certain standard of education and a sense of responsibility. Obviously these were qualities only seen to be possessed by officers.

There was a report from Major General Henchard to the chief of the Imperial Staff on the bombing carried out during the month of October. At the beginning of the month a bombing squadron was ordered to Nancy in north-east France. Owing to bad weather some did not arrive until the middle of the month. Another squadron was ordered there on the 11th, and again due to bad weather, only five aircraft found their way there.

There was a report from the No. 1 Squadron on its journey. It stated that all machines were moved by air under the most difficult conditions. There were continuous low clouds and high winds. The squadron took eleven days to reach Ochey, in north-east France, due to it only being possible to move from one aerodrome to another during clear intervals. By the 15th there were eighteen FE2bs of No. 100 Squadron, fifteen de Havilland 4s of No. 55 Squadron, and the rest were still en route. There were also ten Handley Page aircraft from No. 21 Squadron.

Naval squadrons left on the 15th, spent a day in Paris and arrived on the 17th. It was difficult to form the naval machines into a squadron as all the machines had come from different stations. They had never seen each other before reaching Ochey Aerodrome. It then took the pilots a few days to become familiar with the countryside around them.

The first raid took place on the 17th on factories at Saarbrücken. Two waves of six aircraft took part. All returned safely. These were from No. 55 Squadron.

The next planned raid had to be cancelled because of difficulties with the French at the aerodrome. The French always took off in the same direction, whatever way the wind was blowing. The British machines had problems with this and eventually the aerodrome was divided in two. On the 21st, twelve machines of No. 55 Squadron went to bomb factories and railway lines near Bous and Wadgasson in Saarland, in Germany. One aircraft returned due to engine trouble, the other eleven reached the target. Only ten of these made it back; the other was thought to have landed with engine trouble near the German lines.

On the 24th, nine Handley Page bombers of A Naval Squadron left the aerodrome in the early evening to bomb Saarbrücken. A little later, sixteen aircraft of No. 100 Squadron left to take part in a raid nearer home, near Falkenburg (then in Germany but now in Poland). The first raiders dropped eighty-four 112lb bombs. The second raiders dropped thirteen 230lb bombs and fifteen 25lb bombs.

The weather took a turn for the worse and two of the first group of raiders did not return. One landed in a wood, destroying the aircraft but the crew were unhurt. The second raiding group also lost two machines and the others had problems finding their way back, including one who landed elsewhere and returned later.

This Handley Page bomber seems to be under repair as the propeller on the right-hand engine is missing.

Another raid was carried out on the 30th, when twelve FE2bs of No. 100 Squadron attacked steel works and the station at Volkingham. Nine 230lb bombs and twenty-eight 25lb bombs were dropped. One 230lb bomb hit a train in the Saar Valley, on the borders of France and Germany. There were also 1,150 rounds fired from machine guns. All the aircraft returned safely.

The enemy defences against bombing consisted of numerous anti-aircraft guns, which were fairly accurate. There were also large numbers of searchlights, the operators of which were very alert. There were, surprisingly, very few German aircraft used in defence of the targets.

It wasn't only German airships that came to grief during raids. There was an attempt to bomb Calais in early November using Gothas. One of the aircraft either broke down or was damaged in some way before getting lost in a sea fog and crashing into the chalk cliff of Cape Blanc Nez on the coast of northern France. The aircraft then fell into the sea, which was at high tide, causing the three-man crew to drown.

There was a meeting of the Air Policy Committee in Whitehall in early November. They asked General Trenchard to inform them on the situation in France. He told them that British aircraft were operating further back than they had been. This was because they had not enough aircraft to carry out a good aerial offensive. He claimed that in November 1916 he had eighty-six squadrons of aircraft but by the end of the year, had only fifty-four.

He also complained that the types of aircraft sent out to France were not what they had asked for and their specifications had been ignored. They had asked for machines with two and a half to three hours' flying time, whereas machines with a petrol range of fewer than two hours were sent. The Dolphin had been fitted with four guns instead of three and the added weight of the extra gun cut down on its petrol time.

Commodore Paine argued that this was incorrect and that the specifications asked for by the RFC were discussed and complied with as far as possible. In some cases they had asked for things that were impossible to supply, such as machines that would fly at 130 to 140 miles per hour.

General Trenchard also stated that there was a shortage of suitable ground for aerodromes. Twenty-five aerodromes were being prepared near Nancy and forty aerodromes were being prepared in the British Zone. The French had refused to give them any more prepared aerodromes but had lent them two. Some of the ground had been given to the Americans but as they had not started work on the aerodromes it had been given back to the British.

General Trenchard suggested that squadrons of Handley Page bombers, either naval or army, should finish their training under Captain Lambo in France. He had discussed the matter of a second in command with Douglas Haig, who agreed that in war that was impossible. He said that one mind and one brain must direct all the bombing.

The French would have two night and two day bombing groups ready by April. The plan was to have twenty-five bombing squadrons – seventeen day and eight night squadrons – ready in the near future, eventually building up to thirty – twenty day and ten night squadrons – later on.

General Trenchard also asked that a machine to supersede the DH9 be made available. He explained that the DH9 was not designed as a bomber but was being used as such. Sir William Weir replied that such machines, the DH10, would not be available until July 1919 and would only be slightly better than the DH9.

General Trenchard also gave some details on the latest German aircraft, the new all-metal Junkers, the Halberstadt two-seater and multiple engine machines. The Germans tended to have eight machines in a flight and attach one of the two Junkers fighters to a squadron for protection. It was estimated that in 1918 the Germans would have 4,000 aircraft on the front. By then the British would have 2,000 and the French 3,000.

This crashed British aircraft is arousing a lot of interest amongst the large number of German officers.

At the end of November, General Trenchard sent a report of the work carried out by the RFC during the month to the War Cabinet. Due to the bad weather the number of flying hours was down on the previous month. In October the hours flown were 30,604 but in November it was only 17,716. On some days flying did take place but at a very low altitude, which improved the RFC's conception of what an aircraft could do.

The low flying enabled the pilots to co-operate with the infantry and the tanks and to attack enemy infantry, cavalry and guns with both bombs and machine guns. Due to the low flying, however, losses were heavy at times, with twenty-two machines lost on two days alone. An aircraft hit at low height did not have sufficient altitude to enable it to glide back to base. Sixty-two were lost in total for the month.

There were seventy-four bombing raids and 2,742 bombs were dropped— a weight of 55½ tons. Only 389 enemy bombs had been reported dropped. One of the raids was carried out by twelve aircraft of No. 55 Squadron against the works at Kaiserslautern, which was 100 miles from the aerodrome. Three 230lb bombs and six 112lb bombs were dropped from a height of 15,000 feet. All aircraft returned safely but low cloud stopped the results from being seen.

General Trenchard's report contained some personal pilots' reports, such as the following from Lieutenant H. Taylor of No. 68 Squadron RFC:

While engaging the enemy in the trenches from 30 feet he had his machine badly damaged by machine-gun fire and was forced to land in no-man's-land. He crawled out of his machine, which had lost both wings, and was fired at by German snipers. He took up a German rifle and fired back and eventually made his way to a British patrol, where he assisted in bringing back wounded men. He then found another aircraft from his squadron. The pilot had been wounded and forced to land. Lieutenant Taylor tried to start the machine but the petrol tank had been shot through. He then came home in a staff car.

Another report was from Captain Lee of No. 46 Squadron:

Dropped four bombs on Bourlon Wood. The bursts were difficult to observe owing to heavy shell fire but he believed that two hit their objectives. He then fired at German infantry in Fontaine Village. While retiring temporarily to clear a jammed gun a shell burst and damaged his aircraft and he had to land. He was so close to the German lines that he had to run 100 yards and could not destroy his machine. A shell burst, then blew him across the road. He then helped stretcher bearers bring back wounded.

The last report was of how many enemy machines were brought down in one day by one aircraft. It was flown by Captain A.E. McKeever MC, pilot, and Second Lieutenant L.A. Powell MC, observer:

When flying in a northerly direction nine enemy machines appeared out of the mist on our right side. I made a sharp turn east to get under them and engaged one hostile machine at 15 yards, firing about ten rounds. A minute later, the machine burst into flames on the ground.

As I turned to get back to our lines five enemy aircraft dived on my tail, all firing. My observer fired at one enemy machine at a 20-yard range and this machine fell to the ground and crashed. He engaged two other enemy machines with indecisive results.

I then engaged another machine, which had overshot us, and fired twenty-five rounds at 25 yards range. The enemy machine crashed to the ground. I also engaged two other enemy machines, with indecisive results. My observer's gun had a stoppage and I fought these two machines to within 20 feet of the ground.

When at 100 feet from the ground, the two German machines were still firing, so I dived and, evidently thinking they had got away, they began to climb again and we got back to the lines at about 20 feet.

The raids in December were also affected by the weather. On 5 December, two formations of six de Havilland 4s left at 10.35 and 10.40 am. The objective was the chemical works at Ludwigshafen in Rhineland–Palatinate. One aircraft returned with a petrol blockage. It took the aircraft three hours to reach a point 5 miles south of Kaiserslautern due to high winds. There was also thick mist over the Rhine Valley so the leader decided to abort the mission.

Instead, one formation attacked the railway station and sidings at Zweibrücken and dropped twelve 112lb bombs from 13,500 feet. The second formation attacked the factories immediately west of Saarbrücken, dropping eight 112lb bombs and eight 25lb bombs. This was from 12,000 feet. Four of the bursts were observed to occur in the town.

There was anti-aircraft fire and two machines were damaged and an observer wounded. Four enemy aircraft were seen but did not attack the bombers. The report on the raids also mentioned that due to the intense cold the camera and the oxygen apparatus froze, as did the observers' gun mountings. The pilots and observers, however, were not affected by the cold due to the new type of flying clothing recently issued.

It is interesting to note that although there was severe criticism of German raids in England because they killed civilians, many of the bombs from Allied raids also fell on towns and must have led to civilian causalities as well.

On the 6th, twelve de Havilland 4s left Ochey at 11.30 am to bomb the factories around Saarbrücken, which seems to have been a popular target. One machine had to return because of engine trouble. The others flew almost the whole way over clouds. The target was clear and eight 112lb bombs, eight 25lb bombs and one 230lb bomb were dropped. These caused several fires in factories and in the town.

There was heavy anti-aircraft fire, which did not hit any of the aircraft. Also, eight enemy aircraft were seen but were unable to climb high enough to attack. They then followed the bombers home but did not attempt to attack.

Anti-aircraft guns have developed a long way from the early Lewis guns on stands.

The RNAS had a great deal to do with fighting the air war but also performed other important tasks. One of these was keeping an eye on the weather. To do this they had the latest equipment available, including a device to detect electrical disturbance in the air. This could supposedly detect a storm at extreme distances.

Predicting the weather was of extreme importance to those involved in flying. As well as the high-tech equipment of the time the RNAS also used more basic equipment, such as balloons, to measure wind speeds at high altitude.

Nineteen-eighteen

The beginning of 1918 was to see the difference between the two opposing forces become more marked. The Allies had raw materials from all over the world available to them. The Germans were managing with less and less.

March saw one of the largest dogfights of the war when, on the 18th over Bohain, fifty to sixty enemy aircraft and thirty-eight Allied aircraft got into a fight. The enemy had Albatross and Fokker Triplanes, including Richthofen's Circus. (Richthofen's Circus, or The Flying Circus, as it was also known, was Jagdgeschwader 1, which combined Jastas 4, 6, 10 and 11. It was so called because of the bright colours of its aircraft and the way it followed Allied air activity, moving like a circus train and setting up in tents wherever it needed a base.)

According to German sources the fight involved around forty Allied aircraft flying from the direction of Saint-Quentin in northern France. They were attacked by thirty German aircraft, and a large number of Allied aircraft were shot down whilst the Germans lost none.

There was a plan to repeat the large fight, with sixty British fighters ready to attack the Germans using bombers as bait to tempt them out. However, bad weather put a stop to the plan.

While bombing at night it was impossible for the bomber crews to accurately record what damage was done as they could not see it. Daytime raids, however, were a different matter and the results of raids were meant to be recorded. This was not always possible due to the difficulty of carrying out their duties while bombing. To overcome this, photographs of the results of the raid were often taken instead of reports being made.

Many of the daytime raids were undertaken against targets such as ammunition dumps, military bases and airfields behind enemy lines. A number of these took place at very low altitudes, ignoring the danger of German anti-aircraft fire. They used different bombs for various targets. The lighter bombs were for use against troops while the heavier bombs were used against larger targets such as aerodromes and factories.

There were other problems occupying pilots' attention apart from recording bomb damage. As aircraft flew higher the pilots had problems with lack of oxygen. Some had to be given oxygen when they landed. What was to happen next was even more serious.

With the war on the Russian front over and the Americans expected to arrive soon, the Germans made a desperate last attempt to win the war with a huge attack in March. The German advance was so successful that it pushed the British back in the largest movement since the stalemate of trench warfare had begun.

The German troops that were about to attack were hidden from the Allies, along with German aircraft. From 20 March, the German fliers did their best to stop any Allied recognizance that would spot the build-up of ground forces. The attack began on the 21st – a day when low cloud prevented Allied aircraft from spotting what was going on.

For the first few days it seemed as if the British fliers were more concerned with retreating away from the German advance than combating it. It wasn't until the 24th that they began to appear in large numbers. The work of the pilots became more concentrated on attacking the German ground forces. Because of this most aircraft that were shot down were now being lost to ground fire. To combat fire from below some pilots used flattened steel helmets as seats to protect themselves from bullets from the ground.

Meanwhile, the number of Allied aircraft attacking German supply lines increased. As well as British and French forces, American aircraft were also arriving at the front. The air attacks often devastated the rail heads where the enemy supplies were coming from. It was not the advancing German Army that the Allied air forces attacked but the supply lines, which then cut the advancing forces off from the supplies they needed to keep the push going.

The German aircraft were acting quite differently and were attacking the retreating Allies, often wasting time against small already cut-off forces. It was only later that the German aviators realized their mistake and began trying to defend their supply lines.

The German fliers did their best to stop the Allied attacks. Manfred von Richthofen achieved four victories in these few days, taking him up to seventy. The German Air Service also moved forward with their ground troops and took over evacuated British airfields, often finding much-needed abandoned supplies when they arrived. The British airmen were retreating, as they had done in 1914, as the front line moved back.

By the time the German airmen began trying to defend their supply lines it was already too late. They were eventually overwhelmed by supporting Allied forces and huge numbers of German aircraft were lost.

British aircraft did not escape lightly either. Lieutenant William John Shorter had been in the 1/8th Battalion of the Essex Regiment in 1915-16. He then transferred to the RFC. In March 1918 he managed to land a badly-damaged aircraft at an airfield near Arras in northern France. Two days later, on 24 March 1918, he was killed while flying a Sopwith Camel over German lines. He was twenty years of age – one of many pilots to die when the end of the war was in sight.

The German attack did eventually come to a halt after a few weeks and the failure was to be the last hope of the Germans winning the war. There was also more bad news for the enemy in April when the Red Baron, Manfred von Richthofen, was killed. It was claimed that he was brought down by a Canadian pilot, Captain Roy Brown, from the RNAS. However, it was also thought that machine gunners from the Australian Field Artillery might have been responsible for his downfall. It seems that he may have already been hit and his aircraft disabled when the Canadian pilot fired on him and killed him. His body was laid in state in a hangar in Bertangles, north of Amiens, in France. The Red Baron had eighty kills to his credit.

There were important developments in 1918. An air ministry was finally formed, with Lord Rothermere as Air Minister. One of the first steps taken was to amalgamate the RFC and the RNAS into the RAF from 1 April. Many of the members of both forces were unhappy with this. So were the Germans, who stepped up production of aircraft, expecting the new air minister to do the same. However, there was no way the Germans could still compete with the number of Allied aircraft being produced. The German pilots did not stop fighting, despite the unequal odds.

The battles went on until the final days of the conflict and the RAF were now playing their part. On the second day of the Battle of St Quentin Canal in September 1918, troops at Bellicourt had to know whether an enemy attack was planned. The only way to find out was for an airman and his observer to have a look. They found 3,000 German troops massed in a sunken road ready to advance. They did what the air forces had been doing throughout the war and directed artillery fire onto the German forces, who then withdrew.

By November 1918 and the end of the war, the RAF had 27,000 officers and 290,000 Other Ranks. They also had 22,000 aircraft. They had come a long way from the days of the Air Battalion. It may have taken much longer than was needed to turn the air services into a modern air force but it had finally happened. The aircraft that the RAF were flying had also come a long way since the outbreak of hostilities. There is no doubt that the progress in flying and aircraft design between 1914 and 1918 had been so rapid because of the war.

The end of the war was to signal danger for the newly formed service. The cuts forced on the armed services due to the outbreak of peace were to hit the RAF hard. It seemed as if it was to lose its short-lived independence. When Winston Churchill became Minister for War in the election after the end of the conflict, he was also given responsibility for Air, as its independence was no longer seen to be important.

Luckily for the RAF, Churchill was a keen supporter of air power, having learnt to fly himself. He reappointed Hugh Trenchard as Chief of Air Staff, a post he then held until 1929. Trenchard's Memorandum of December 1919 called for an independent peacetime air force that should concentrate on training and the development of navigation, metrology and wireless communication.

In spite of Churchill and Trenchard's support of the RAF, the service was hit badly by cuts. By 1920, there were fewer than 30,000 members left in service and the WRAF had been completely disbanded. However, there were some developments in its favour. The Royal Air Force College at Cranwell opened in 1920 and the RAF Staff College in Andover opened in 1921.

Even though the government's interest in an independent air force was waning, there was interest from other directions. Now the war was over the Navy and the Army both hoped to regain control over their parts of the air service, in spite of the problems that had been evident throughout the war. The dispute led to further creation of numerous government committees to discuss the issue; history was repeating itself.

The RAF did manage to retain its independence, thanks in no small measure to Trenchard. Churchill helped but after a few years had moved on to other government departments. Eventually, there was to be a measure of giving in to the Navy when the Fleet Air Arm was formed in 1924, seeing aircraft based on naval ships, and in 1937, this was placed under naval control.

One of the ways the RAF showed its worth in the post-war period was in policing the Empire. It was a convenient way of keeping control of the large areas covered by the Empire and was also to prove much cheaper than using land forces.

In 1920, the RAF were instrumental in aiding land forces to subdue rebels in Somaliland. In 1921, they were given responsibility for policing tribal unrest in Iraq. In 1928, the RAF were responsible for the first evacuation of civilians when they rescued diplomatic staff cut off by civil war in Afghanistan.

Many of the aircraft factories that had operated during the First World War were closed when peace came. The RAF continued to use many of the aircraft that had flown into battle during the conflict. Some newer, more modern aircraft were also ordered, often from those companies that had supplied aircraft before.

A new bomber, the Avro Aldershot, was a single-engined aircraft that was supplied to the RAF just after the war; it could carry a bomb load equal to the earlier twin-engined bombers. It finally came into service in the mid 1920s, but after a few years the RAF decided to scrap single-engined bombers.

Another well-known name supplied a twin-engined bomber at the time that the Aldershot was on its way out of use. The Handley Page Hyderabad was a military version of the company's commercial airliner. Again, the aircraft did not last long and was phased out by the mid 1930s.

Other bombers used during the inter-war period included the Vickers Virginia, the Handley Page Hinaldi and Heyford, all biplanes. The mid-1930s began to see the use of monoplanes such as the Fairy Hendon and the Handley Page Harrow.

Fighter development tended to stagnate during the inter-war period as there didn't seem to be as much need for them as there was for bombers. Many of the wartime fighters continued to be used and any new aircraft were often improved versions of them. Biplanes were to be the norm for some time to come.

One of the first post-war fighters ordered by the RAF was the Armstrong Whitworth Siskin. It wasn't a great success until its original Dragonfly engine was replaced with the Jaguar. The Siskin III also later became the first all-metal fighter aircraft used by the RAF. New engines and the takeover of smaller companies were to lead to further development of fighter aircraft.

Another fighter that was the result of a new engine and the takeover of a First World War aircraft company was the Gloster Nightjar, or Mars X. It was originally called the Nieuport Nighthawk, with a Dragonfly engine. When Nieuport were taken over by the Gloster Aircraft Company in 1920, they changed the Dragonfly engine for a Bentley and altered the aircraft's name. The Nightjar was intended as a replacement for the Sopwith Camel on aircraft carriers but it was never ordered in any great numbers.

The use of biplanes as fighters was to continue for some time. The first single-wing fighter used by the RAF was a development of what was to be called the Fury Monoplane made by Hawker in the mid 1930s. Before the design was complete a new Rolls-Royce engine was developed, the Merlin. The Fury was redesigned to take this engine and it became the Hurricane.

The expansion of the RAF and the development of a number of new aircraft was to happen eventually. As it had in the past, this was the result of a new threat and then a new war. The approach of the Second World War proved that there had indeed been a need for an independent air force.

First World War Airfields in Britain

Andover, Hampshire
Bicester, Oxfordshire
Biggin Hill, Kent
Brooklands, Surrey
Burnham-on-Crouch, Essex
Castle Bromwich, Warwickshire
Catterick, Yorkshire
Chingford, Essex
Chattis Hill, Hampshire
Cranwell, Lincolnshire
Doncaster, Yorkshire
Duxford, Cambridgeshire
Eastchurch, Kent
Eastleigh, Hampshire
Elsham Wolds, Lincolnshire
Fairlop, Essex
Farnborough, Hampshire
Felixstowe, Suffolk
Finningley, Yorkshire
Ford, Sussex
Fowlmere, Cambridgeshire
Goldhanger, Essex
Goldington, Bedfordshire
Gosport, Hampshire
Grantham, Lincolnshire
Great Yarmouth, Norfolk
Hainault, Essex
Halton, Buckinghamshire
Harlaxton, Lincolnshire
Hemswell, Lincolnshire
Hendon, London

Henlow, Bedfordshire
Hornchurch, Essex
Hounslow, London
Lakenheath, Suffolk
Larkhill, Wiltshire
Manston, Kent
Marham, Norfolk
Martlesham Heath, Suffolk
Mona, Anglesey
Molesworth, Cambridgeshire
Mousehold Heath, Norfolk
Narborough, Norfolk
Netheravon, Wiltshire
Northolt, London
North Weald, Essex
Orford Ness, Suffolk
Old Sarum, Wiltshire
Penhurst, Kent
Perton, Staffordshire
Portholme Meadow, Cambridgeshire
Pulham, Norfolk
Shawbury, Shropshire
Southend, Essex
Stow Maries, Essex
Upavon, Wiltshire
Upper Heyford, Oxfordshire
Usworth, Durham
Waddington, Lincolnshire
Wyton, Cambridgeshire
Yatesbury, Wiltshire

Appendix 2

Early Aircraft Manufacturers in Britain

Many of the names listed were the same companies that changed their names at various times in their existence. More details can be found in Chapter 2.

Aeronautical Syndicate Ltd., Hendon, London
Air Navigation & Engineering Company, Surrey
Aircraft Manufacturing Company, Hendon, London
Airships Ltd., Hendon, London
Alliance Aeroplane Company Ltd., London
Ariel Manufacturing Company Ltd., Hendon, London
Armstrong, Whitworth & Company Ltd., Newcastle, Northumberland
(now Tyne & Wear)
Austin Motor Company, Birmingham
Avro & Company Ltd., Manchester
Barclay, Curle & Company Ltd., Glasgow
Beadmore & Company Ltd., Dumbartonshire
Blackburn Aeroplane and Motor Company, Leeds
Blériot Manufacturing Aircraft Company, Addlestone, Surrey
Blériot & Spad, Addlestone, Surrey
Boulton & Paul Ltd., Norwich, Norfolk
Breuget Aeroplanes, London
Bristol Aeroplane Co., Bristol
British and Colonial Aeroplane Company, Bristol
Brush Electrical Engineering Company, Loughborough, Leicestershire
Clayton and Shuttleworth. London
Cody, Farnborough, Hampshire
Coventry Ordnance Company, Coventry, Warwickshire
Daimler Company, Coventry, Warwickshire
Denny & Brothers, Dumbarton
D. Napier & Sons, London
Dudbridge Ironworks, Stroud, Gloucestershire

Eastbourne Aviation Company Ltd., Eastbourne, Sussex
English Electric, Bradford, Yorkshire
ENV Engines, Sheffield, Yorkshire, and Willesden, London
Fairey Aviation Company Ltd., Hayes, Middlesex
Frederick Sage & Company, London
G & J Weir, Glasgow
Grahame-White Aviation Company Ltd., Hendon, London
Handley Page Ltd., Barking & Cricklewood, London
Hewlett & Blondeau Ltd., London
Howard Flanders Ltd., Richmond, London
Howard T. Wright, London
Humber Ltd., Coventry, Warwickshire
Joucques Aviation Works, London
J. Samuel White & Company, Cowes, Isle of Wight
Kingsbury Aviation Company Ltd., London
Mann Egerton & Company Ltd., Norwich, Norfolk
Martin & Handasyde, Brooklands, Surrey
May Harden & May, Hythe, Kent
Morgan & Company, Leighton Buzzard, Bedfordshire
Napier & Sons, London
National Aircraft Company, Surrey
Norman Thompson Flight Company, Middleton-on-Sea, Sussex
Oakley Ltd., Ilford, Essex
Parnell & Sons Ltd., Bristol
Peter Hooker Ltd., Walthamstow, London
Phoenix Dynamo Manufacturing Company Ltd., Bradford, Yorkshire
Piggott Brothers & Company Ltd., London
Portholme Aerodrome Ltd., Huntingdon, Huntingdonshire
Robey & Company, London
Royal Aircraft Company, Farnborough, Hampshire
Ruston Procter & Company Ltd., Lincoln
Savages Ltd., King's Lynn, Norfolk
S. E. Saunders Ltd., Isle of Wight
Short Brothers, Rochester, Kent
Sopwith Aviation Company, Kingston upon Thames, Surrey
Standard Motor Company, Coventry, Warwickshire
Sunbeam Motor Car Company, Wolverhampton, Staffordshire
Vickers Ltd., London

Wells Aviation Company Ltd., London
Westland Aircraft Works, Yeovil, Somerset
Whitehead Aircraft Factory, Richmond, Surrey
Wolseley Motors Ltd., Birmingham

Aviation Museums and Collections in Britain

Avro Heritage Centre, Woodford Aerodrome, Chester Road, Woodford, Cheshire SK7 1QR
www.avroheritage.com

Battle of Britain Memorial, Capel-le-Ferne, Kent
www.battleofbritainmemorial.org

Battle of Britain Memorial Flight Visitor Centre, RAF Conninsgby, Lincoln LN4 4SY
www.raf.mod.uk/bbmf

Bentwaters Cold War Museum, Building 134, Bentwaters Parks, Rendlesham, Woodbridge, Suffolk IP12 2TW
www.bcwrn.org.uk

Berkshire Museum of Aviation, Mohawk Way, Woodley, Berkshire RG5 4UE,
www.museumofberkshireaviation.co.uk

95th Bomb Group Heritage Association Museum, The Red Feather Club, Horham, Suffolk IP21 5DG
www.95thbg-horham.com

100th Bomb Group Museum, Common Road, Dickelburgh, Diss, Norfolk IP21 4PH
www.100bgmus.org.uk

Boscombe Down Aviation Collection, Hanger 1, Old Sarum Airfield, Old Sarum, Salisbury, Wiltshire SP4 6DZ
www.boscombedownaviationcollection.co.uk

Bottisham Airfield Museum, The Royal British Legion, 31 Downing Close, Bottisham, Cambridgeshire CB25 9DD
www.bottishamairfieldmuseum.org.uk

Bournmouth Aviation Museum, Merritown Lane, Hurn, Christchurch, Dorset BH23 6BA
www.aviation-museum.co.uk

Boxted Airfield Museum, Langham Lane, Langham, Essex CO4 5NW
www.boxted-airfield.com

Breznett Aeronautical Museum, Ivychurch Road, Romney Marsh, Kent TN29 0EE
www.breznettaero.co.uk

Bristol Aero Collection, Hanger 2, Kemble Airfield, Cirencester, Gloucestershire GL6 7BQ
www.bristolaero.com

British Airways Heritage Collection, Building 387, Heathrow Airport, Hounslow, Middlesex TW6 2JA
www.bamuseum.com

Brooklands Museum, Brooklands Road, Weybridge, Surrey KT13 0QN
www.brooklandsmuseum.com

Croydon Airport Visitor Centre, Airport House, Purley Way, Croydon, Surrey CR0 0XZ
www.croydonairport.org.uk

Davidstow Airfield and Cornwall at War Museum, Nottier Park, Davidstow, Camelford, Cornwall PL32 9YF
www.cornwallatwarmuseum.co.uk

De Havilland Heritage Centre, Salisbury Hall, London Colney, Hertfordshire AL2 1EX
www.dehavillandmuseum.co.uk

Dunkswell Memorial Museum, Flightway Business Park, Unit 4, Dunksewell, nr Honiton, Devon EX14 5RD
www.dunkeswellmemorialmuseum.org.uk

East Essex Aviation Museum, The Martello Tower, Point Clear Caravan Park, Clacton-on-Sea, Essex CO16 8LJ
www.eastessexaviationsociety.org

Farnborough Air Services Trust, Trenchard House, 85 Farnborough Road, Hampshire GU14 6TF
www.airsciences.org.uk/museum.html

Fenland and West Norfolk Aviation Museum, Old Lynn Road, West Walton Highway, Wisbech, Cambridgeshire PE14 7DA
www.aeroflight.co.uk

Fleet Air Arm Museum, RNAS Yeoviltown, Ilchester, Somerset BA22 8HT
www.fleetairarm.com

Gatwick Aviation Museum, Lowfield Heath Road, Charlwood, Surrey RH6 0BT
www.gatwick-aviation-museum.co.uk

Hunter Flying Club, Exeter International Airport, Exeter, Devon EX5 2BD
www.classicjets.co.uk

Imperial War Museum Duxford, Duxford, Cambridgeshire CB22 4QR
www.iwm.org.uk/duxford

Imperial War Museum London, Lambeth Road, London SE1 6HZ
www.London.iwm.org.uk

Imperial War Museum North, Trafford Wharf Road, Trafford Park, Manchester M17 1TZ
www.north.iwm.org.uk

Kent Battle of Britain Museum, Aerodrome Road, Hawkinge, Kent
CT18 7AG
www.kbobm.org

Lashenden Air Warfare Museum, Headcorn Aeriodrome, Ashford, Kent
TN27 9HX
www.lashendenairwarfremuseum

Lincolnshire Aviation Heritage Centre, The Airfield, East Kirkby,
Lincolnshire PE23 4DE
www.lincsaviation.co.uk

Manx Aviation and Military Museum, Ronaldsway Airport, Ballasalla,
Isle of Man IM9 2AT
www.maps.iofm.net

Martlesham Heath Control Tower Museum, Parker's Place, Eagle Way,
Martlesham Heath, Suffolk IP5 3UZ
www.mhas.org.uk

Medway Aircraft Preservation Society, Rochester Airport, Chatham,
Kent ME5 9SD
www.mapsi.co.uk

Midland Air Museum, Coventry Airport, Baginton, Coventry, Warks
CV8 3AZ
www.midlandairmuseum.co.uk

Montrose Air Station Heritage Centre, Waldron Road, Montrose, Angus
DD10 9BB
www.rafmontrose.org.uk

Muckleburgh Collection, Weybourne Camp, Weybourne, Norfolk NR25
7EG
www.muckleburgh.co.uk

Museum of Army Flying, Middle Wallop, Stockbridge, Hampshire SO20
8DY
www.flying-museum.org.uk

Museum of Flight, East Fortune Airfield, East Lothian EH39 5LF
www.nms.ac.uk

Norfolk and Suffolk Aviation Museum, The Street, Flixton, Suffolk NR35 1NZ
www.aviationmuseum.net

North Weald Airfield Museum, Ad Astra House, Hurricane Way, North Weald Aerodrome, Epping, Essex CM16 6AA
www.northwealdairfieldhistory.org

Norwich Aviation Museum, Old Norwich Road, Horsham St Faith, Norwich, Norfolk NR10 3JF
www.cnam.co.uk

Parham Airfield Museum, Parham, Framlingham, Suffolk IP13 9AF
www.parhamairfieldmuseum.co.uk

Purfleet Heritage Centre, River Court, Centurion Way, Purfleet, Essex RM19 1ZY
www.purfleet-heritage.com

RAF Museum Cosford, Cosford, Shifnal, Shropshire TF11 8UP
www.rafmuseum.org.uk/cosford

RAF Manston History Museum, Manston Road, Ramsgate, Kent CT12 5DF
www.rafmanston.co.uk

RAF Oulton Museum, Blickling Estate, Blickling, nr Norwich, Norfolk NR11 6NF
wwwnationaltrust.org.uk

RAF Wickenby Memorial Collection, Wickenby Aerodrome, The Control Tower, Langworth, Lincolnshire LN3 5AX
www.rafwmm.flyer.co.uk

Royal Airforce Museum, RAF Museum, Hendon, London NW9 5LL
www.rafmuseum.org.uk

Science Museum, Exhibition Road, South Kensington, London SW7 2DD
www.sciencemuseumstore.com

Shoreham Aircraft Museum, High Street, Shoreham Village, Sevenoaks, Kent TN14 7TB
www.shoreham-aircraft-museum.co.uk

Solent Sky Museum, Albert Road South, Southampton, Hampshire SO14 3FR
www.spitfireonline.co.uk

Tangmere Military Aviation Museum, Tangmere Airfield, Chichester, West Sussex PO20 6ES
www.tangmere-museum.org.uk

Trenchard Museum, RAF Halton Camp, Buckinghamshire HP22 5PG
www.trenchardmuseum.org.uk

Yorkshire Air Museum, Halifax Way, Elvington, York YO41 4AU
www.yorkshireairmuseum.co.uk

Wellington Aviation Museum and Gallery, British School House, Moreton-in-Marsh, Gloucestershire GL56 0BG
www.wellingtonaviation.org

Wings Museum, Unit 1, Bucklands Farm, Balcombe, West Sussex RH17 6JT
www.wingsmuseum.co.uk

Sources and Bibliography

Books

Baring, M., *Flying Corps Headquarters 1914-1918*, William Blackwood & Sons, London, 1968.

Barker, R., *The Royal Flying Corps in World War One*, Constable and Robinson, London, 1995.

Bartlett, C.P.O. DSC, *Bomber Pilot 1916-18*, Ian Allan, London, 1974.

Bills, L.W., *A Medal for Life*, Spellmount, Stroud, Gloucestershire, 1990.

Brooke-Smith, P.W.L., *History of Early British Military Aeronautics*, privately published, 1952.

Cronin, D,. *Royal Navy Shipboard Aircraft Developments 1912-1931*, Air Britain, Woodbridge, Suffolk, 1990.

Crosby, F., *Bombers of World Wars One and Two*, Anness Publishing, London, 2005.

Davis, M., *Airco*, Crowood, Marlborough, Wiltshire, 2001.

Franks, N., *Sopwith Triplane Aces of World War One*, Osprey, Oxford, 2004.

Frater, A., *The Balloon Factory*, Picador, London, 2008.

Gamble, C.F.S., *The Story of a North Sea Air Station*, Oxford University Press, 1928.

Harris, Sherwood, *The First to Fly*, Tab Aero, London, 1991.

Hayzlett, J. (translator), *Hunting with Richthofen*, Grub Street, London, 1998.

Hoffman, Paul, *Wings of Madness*, Harper Perennial, London, 2004.

Lewis, C., *Sagittarius Rising*, Peter Davies, London, 1936.

Miller, James, Cranfield, H.S., & Plowman, W., *The People's War Book: A Cyclopedia and Chronology of the Great War and Canada's Part in it*, R.C. Barnum & Co, Cleveland, 1920.

Smith, G., *Essex and its Race for the Skies*, Countryside Books, Newbury, Berkshire, 2007.

Treadwell, T., *British and Allied Aircraft Manufacturers of the First World War*, Amberley, Stroud, Gloucestershire, 2011.

West, Jack, *Personal Memories of Dagenham Village: 1920 Onwards*, republished Arthur H. Stockwell Ltd., Ilfracombe, 1993.

Imperial War Museum Documents

Private Papers of Harold Hillier RFC.
Private Papers of Lieutenant C.E. Young RFC.

Private Papers of Lieutenant H.T. Kemp RFC.
Private Papers of L.I. Howden RFC.
Private Papers of W.I. Prothero RFC.
Private Papers of E.J. Broady RNAS.
Private Papers of Captain T.B. Williams RNAS.
Private Papers of W.C. Knight RNAS.
Private Papers of Wing Commander L. Howard Wilkins DSC RNAS.

National Archive Documents

CAB/23/3-0041
CAB/23/3-0071
CAB/23/4
CAB/24/2-0009
CAB/24/2-0029
CAB/24/2-0031
CAB/24/2-0037
CAB/24/2-0052
CAB/24/3-0031
CAB/24/6
CAB/24/7
CAB/24/10
CAB/24/15-0037
CAB/24/17
CAB/24/19
CAB/24/20
CAB/24/22-0029
CAB/24/24-0048
CAB/24/28-0038
CAB/24/28-0060
CAB/24/31-0023
CAB/24/31-0061
CAB/24/34
CAB/24/35
CAB/24/35-0028
CAB/24/42
CAB/24/51
CAB/24/67

Newspapers & Periodicals

Air Britain Digest, Vol 36, No. 6, Nov/Dec 1984.
'Dagenham Days', *The Aeronautical Journal of the Royal Aeronautical Society*,
    Vol 74, February 1970.

Flight magazine: 21 August 1909; 25 September 1909; 29 January 1915; 16 March 1916; 23 March 1916.

New Scientist: 14 April 1977.

The Illustrated War News: 19 July 1916; 9 August 1916; 17 July 1917; 29 August 1917.

The Manchester Guardian: 11 March 1909; 23 September 1909; 25 September 1909; 14 October 1909; 16 October 1909; 25 October 1909; 13 July 1910.

The Penny Illustrated Paper & Illustrated Times: 11 September 1909; 23 October 1909; 30 April 1910.

The Observer: 18 October 1911; 18 February 1912; 24 March 1912; 28 April 1912.

The Times: 10 August 1908; 26 February 1909; 28 March 1910; 13 April 1910; 7 December 1910; 13 February 1911; 12 January 1912; 20 March 1912; 13 April 1912; 16 April 1912; 7 June 1912; 25 December 1912; 8 May 1913; 14 June 1914; 21 June 1915; 18 October 1915; 31 December 1915; 13 September 1916; 8 November 1916; 19 December 1916; 1 June 1917; 17 October 1917; 24 September 1918.

Index